VIEWS OF THE CHURCH
FROM THE LIQUOR STORE

BRANDON C. LOVELACE

ISBN: 148103006X
ISBN 13: 9781481030069
Library of Congress Control Number: 2016901337
CreateSpace Independent Publishing Platform
North Charleston, South Carolina

Dedicated to North Omaha and Gary, Indiana

CONTENTS

THANK YOU

GOD
Sharon Johnson
John Lovelace
Traci Lovelace
Ernest Powell
Andile Mahlangeni-Byndon
Dionte Johnson
Fred Wisdom
Michaela Gunter-Johnson
Margaret (Peggy) Jones
Thedrice Jones
Jerry Freeman
Darius Malone
Allen Nelson
Dr. Michael Eric Dyson
Dr. Cornel West
Judge Daryl Lowe
Ja'Vonte Loud
Christian Griffin
Jamel LeBranch
Erick Dishmon
Brandon Allen

James Boyd
Derrell Bradford
The 100 Black Men of Omaha
The University Nebraska-Omaha
Prince Hall Freemasonary
Brittany Edmonds
Eric Ewing
Henry Atkinson
North Omaha
Gary, Indiana
Lindsey Stennis
Tristan Harper
Shawn Carter
My aunties
My uncles
Cousins
Sisters
Brothers

Christopher Olds
David Love
Adrian Bradford
Brittany McCain
Morgan McCain
Sherman McCain
Timothy Gaskin
Teylor Gaskin
Mikki Humm
Jasmine Ward
Jordan Teamer
Iziah Crawford
Sierra Russell
Jamie Retina
Lexi Talich
Chanera Pierce
Brittany Edmonds
Raheem Sanders
James (Jody) Williams

CHAPTER 1

Views of the Church from the Liquor Store

In his classic song "A Change Gon' Come," Sam Cooke in his eloquent voice sings about living a hard life in a little tent along the river. He speaks of the pain in his community, but he's afraid to die because he is still filled with the audacity of hope that it will get better. Even when he is continually knocked down and told not to come around, Sam Cooke still looks to the sky with a sense of hope.

As I began compiling ideas, thoughts, and a direction that I wanted this book to go in, I began to channel everything that I loved and cared about, along with the things that I despised in my community. One day on my way to Salem Baptist Church on a Sunday morning, I began to notice the amount of liquor stores I passed in North Omaha to get to my destination. I also began to take into account that from almost all the liquor stores that I passed, you could also view a church. Even though churches and alcohol are prevalent in every community, only dilapidated areas of socioeconomic collapse seem to have them in such close proximity.

In retrospect, once I achieved the legal age required to purchase alcohol, I quickly stopped buying it from urban areas—not because I didn't care about spending my money in the black community, but seeing some of the people who frequented these locations was draining on my heart. It wasn't uncommon for me to step outside a liquor store only to be greeted by someone asking for some loose change to buy a bottom-shelf shooter. On the surface one can see a person with a messed-up life who now had nothing better to do than to beg for change, but that's an immature thought because it doesn't take into account the situations that drove that person to the bottle or the predicaments that led to begging for change.

We all have stories, but in a world that seems to be encamped in materialism, those without are deemed not to matter. Those who we deem not to matter are brushed off and placed in a paradigm of failure and trouble. The liquor store can be a symbol of despair, but that view of the church from someone suffering from pauperism is looked at as a beacon of aspiration.

Factually and metaphorically speaking, churches are looked at as symbols of hope, places where people meet people they marry, find out about jobs… They are centers of their morality.

The dichotomy of liquor stores and churches is an interesting one because it's almost a battle of good and evil, and we live in a culture that is obsessed with the politics of winners and losers.

Many conspiracy theorists might argue that liquor stores are strategically in poor black areas to keep those areas oppressed. Even though alcohol abuse does not discriminate among class, race, gender, or sexual orientation, it does tend to be more prevalent in areas of socioeconomic collapse. Communities that have underfunded schools, lack of jobs, and miniscule chances of upward mobility but high rates of crime and unemployment and a high number of liquor stores are present for the residents of these areas.

When I step into church, especially churches that have a rich legacy like Salem, it can almost be an overwhelming experience because you see a wide range of cars in the parking lot, from Hondas to the luxury Mercedes-Benz. Also, you see a high density of high-quality suits worn by the members of the congregation, but the message in the scripture almost always is relevant to the world that exists outside those walls of the church. However, church for most who are believers is more than a sermon and selections from the choir. Whenever I sat in church, I stayed close to the back, and I began to notice that this part of the church is where most of the visitors sat, along with those who didn't attend service on a consistent basis. Even though people worship differently, these people always seemed to shout and praise with more joy than others. It made you wonder what brought them into church on that particular Sunday morning.

When I was growing up, it wasn't uncommon for me to hear church folks express that we are living in the last days because of all the woes and violence, but I always took that statement for face value until I was much older. As a child I would pray nightly until I was probably into my junior high years that GOD would deliver us from gangs and deliver some of my family members from drug abuse. Even at such a young age, I was being socialized within a theological construct to believe that everything evil that occurred was at the irreverent expense of the devil. No one ever took the time to explain the systemic issues that were at play that caused drug abuse, alcoholism, poverty, and disease. We all saw the same image, but the contextual relevance was always hidden or not discussed.

When I sit in the back of these churches and I see people who may be looking for a sense of purpose as they receive the word from their position in the pews, it makes one wonder why they are here. Most of these people whom we shame are coming from a world outside the church that is absent of divinity and is a space of godlessness. It makes you understand the words of Tupac Shakur, on his song *"Only God can Judge me," where he speaks on whether GOD cares about the pain that thugs feel.*

Most people whom we deemed nefarious, like those who hang around in liquor stores, are still looking for a purpose and for the source of their existence, but we are preaching our myopic journey to them instead of listening to their stories about poverty, street gangs, drugs, sexism, racism, and pain.

When we listen to them, then we must address our oppressive behavior that we place upon those we deem less valuable, unequal, less beautiful, ungodly, immoral, and erroneous because of our parochialism, patriarchy, classism, and homophobia that we dress up in respectability politics.

While people from the hegemonic culture inherit businesses, trust funds, nepotism, and bank accounts, many from my community inherit poverty, depleted resources, underfunded schools, and churches that can be viewed from the liquor store.

CHAPTER 2

My Nigga, your Nigger

"**D**id you hear about President Obama using the N-word, Brandon?"

My coworker stopped me in the office to ask my take on the president of the United States using the word *nigger* during a podcast. I simply replied that I had heard it and I asked whether or not she heard the entire podcast or just simply a sound bite. She replied that she only heard the sound bite and how she wanted to eradicate the usage of it from everyone (including black people). This discussion somehow prompted her to ask me whether or not I used that word. I simply replied, "Yes, I use it every day with promiscuity!"

My sudden responses must've shocked her and taken her back, because all she could say was why, after proceeding to tell me why it's such an ugly word and how it was used to dehumanize black people in this country.

I wanted to express to her that it wasn't her place as a white woman, liberal or not, to tell me which words were appropriate or not for my everyday lexicon. Instead I decided to use this as a point in argument for President Obama by saying she wasn't proving his point in the podcast that she failed to listen to thoroughly. President Obama was basically saying that many view racism overtly or in a category of fast terror. While it isn't a categorical mistake, it can be deemed a junior varsity categorical assertion.

While calling black people niggers in exasperating tones and killing minorities in the name of white superiority can be looked at as fast terror, at times it leaves little room for nuance in the conscience of others who tend to ignore the subtle forms of racisms that are professed by those who refuse to acknowledge their racism since they don't use that infamous N-word.

This brief exchange in the office forced me to internally look at why I use the word and why we sweep underlying systemic racism under the rug.

I was in partial agreement with my coworker; I do believe white people and nonblack people should bury that nefarious and odious word from their lexicon. I will never support legislation that would restrict them from using the word, but I would always ask why they would want to use a word that has so much history that they claim we would should move past because of the ugly stain it has left not only on the face of the United States, but on the bodily world.

The term *nigger* simply articulates a vocabulary of terror that encapsulates more than racism in linguistic forms—it symbolizes systemic oppression against blacks educationally, economically, politically, and socially. I would never support legislation that restricts the First Amendment rights of people, not only because of the implications and the precedent it could set forth in the future, but also because it's a waste of time since it doesn't legislate what the word underscores.

My liberal coworker may have come from a genuine place when she gave her assertion on why the word should be eradicated from the linguistic consciousness of the world, but that type of dogmatic suggestion underlines greater issues that many blacks have with white liberals who dress themselves up as allies. I generally hate using the terminology of ally because in a sense it mutes and limits people's voices and participation. While I didn't feel my coworker's opinion was necessary, I allowed her to express herself, even though it resulted in me providing a countervailing narrative to her argument on why the word should be erased.

While she told me in a dogmatic way that she knows the difference between how the white people say it and how some in the black culture use it among their own race, the two distinct differences still didn't sway her opinion on the word. She and many others who fall within her ilk look at present-day America within the constructs of a post-racial utopian society, while many blacks are trying to navigate within this present-day covert dystopia. The dichotomy of America's dream of a post-racial juxtaposed with Black America's racial nightmare is ever present in a place that has still attempted to degrade the black experience.

When I look at the term *nigga* and my usage among other blacks, it is a subtle acknowledgment of others who are have been shrunken by democracy by being told literally and figuratively that their life doesn't matter. That's why I told her I used the term with promiscuity among other black males and females in the struggle. To be a nigger in the hegemonic culture means to have a lack of control of the environment that you occupy. This was a word that was used to dehumanize or scrape away our existence, but now it is used in a manner to connect us as we try to counter the mechanisms thrown at us as a way to subvert us from waking out of this physical nightmare. Once outsiders make an adequate attempt to understand the meaning of how the word has transformed from a racial epithet and into an embracement of love, then they can understand the tradition that is distinctive among black Americans, which allows us to take something that is painful, cruel, and tragic and turn it into a colloquialism of positivity. While it's easy to show how the word notably derived from a place of hate, that shouldn't dismiss the struggle blacks went through to find a solidaric circulating brotherhood of love.

This word does carry a de facto social law that designates its usage for one group juxtaposed to another, but when she suggested that no one use it, she was subconsciously trying to legislate the lives of black folks like many have done before. Instead of trying to garner a broader understanding of the etymology of the word within black circles, she decided to remain in her epistemological closet of parochialism. While it may seem innocent, a white woman trying to legislate language has adverse effects on why the word was transformed within black circles, compared to the goal that she may have tried to accomplish. This works as a machination in terms of challenging the intellectual acuity of black linguistic culture.

We can't have these myopic views regarding what words have to be fixed. The issue doesn't revolve around black people appropriating the word; the issue is that whiteness isn't being allowed to exert its privilege within this space. Whiteness is the global standard, but with this topic it feels as though we have to infantilize them so they can understand the racial politics that circumvent the word.

It's not that black people are ignorant to the rooted history of the etymology of the word *nigger/nigga* that defines a person as ignorant. We are very aware of the pain, trauma, and the legacy of it, but I feel most are ignorant to the history of black people in the United States. We are a group of people who were given scraps that we ended up turning into food that was mixed with soul. So while the word was a deliberate attempt to dehumanize us and channel us into a segment of second-class citizens, black people stood up, flipped the word, and put it in a proverbial lock that's protected from white appropriation.

By refusing to romanticize over a wishbone of hope that maybe they would treat us right if we took on a passive demeanor, some black folk got a backbone and stood up to take back part of their humanity.

CHAPTER 3

WHY MEMORY IS CRITICAL

> *When the whole nation had finished crossing the Jordan, the Lord*
> *said to Joshua, "Choose twelve men from among the people, one*
> *from each tribe, tell them to take up twelve stones from the middle*
> *of the Jordan, from right where the priests are standing, and carry*
> *them over with you and put them down at the place where you stay*
> *tonight." So Joshua called together the twelve men he had appointed*
> *from the Israelites, one from each tribe, and said to them, "Go over*
> *before the ark of the Lord your God into the middle of the Jordan.*
> *Each of you is to take up a stone on his shoulder, according to the*
> *number of the tribes of the Israelites, to serve as a sign among you.*
> *In the future, when your children ask you, 'What do these stones*
> *mean?' tell them that the flow of the Jordan was cut off before the*
> *ark of the covenant of the Lord. When it crossed the Jordan, the*
> *waters of the Jordan were cut off. These stones are to be a memorial*
> *to the people of Israel forever."*
>
> *—Joshua 4:1–7*

The concept of memory is critical because it is a deliberate attempt to focus on ideas and identities to nurture survival in the heart of the struggle. Memory can be considered the bullets that attack the amnesia of the truth. Memory helps foster a sense of history and pride in oneself. Memory is the root of one's foundation, while the present cultivates the new growth of that memory.

The United States in particular is critical of the history it chooses to promote and actively stimulate the masses with, while simultaneously deciding what needs to be forgotten or brushed under the rug. A fecundity of books are released yearly about the founding fathers of this nation, presidents and war heroes, but when it comes to acts such as the United States' original sin, it is just looked at as the past. The United States believes that the ushering of those indigenous people into lands that are impossible to cultivate is a form of adequate restorative justice, but being cognizant of how the United States treats history is important to understanding why the upkeep of black history is important to the growth of black memory.

When it comes to telling the painful narrative of the bloodshed, rape, brutality, and commodification of black cultural identity, we are told to just simply get over that and are expected to adopt a philosophy of benign neglect. The United States loves to teach its rich history of triumph, but wants to ignore blacks in the United States when we stand up and attempt to tell ours.

Black people didn't just get great because the United States became a powerful nation. We as a people had to fight, walk upright, protest, confront oppression, and die by surrendering blood and limbs. Instead, the country wants to tell half-truths and edify the idea that people marched and Lyndon B. Johnson recognized the fight by signing a civil rights bill. We are made to believe that affirmative action, the disembodiment of Jim Crow, and the integration of blacks into US tradition propelled us, but due to US amnesia, they forget that we had preexisting civilizations of greatness before slavery.

This is why memory is critical, not just in the paradigm of an American context, but the global troposphere. We don't have to romanticize about ancient Kemet (modern-day Egypt), but it's important to talk about its greatness. We shouldn't be covered under the candid view of slavery, AIDS, poverty, and cultural deprivation. Instead, we should be conscious of everything. Through anthropological research and findings, we now know that everybody was birthed out of Africa. So when we are depicted as less than equal and unmolested of intellectual virtue, the world has to notice that thinking started with us. While other civilizations were running around in caves, we were birthing logistics and mathematics and welding the fabric of the world.

Just as the scripture that predicated this essay stated, we must get those stones (memory) and show them to the children so that they are familiar with the context of where they came from. We must refuse to accept the notion that we started in docile positions of suffering and failure. We must understand that we come from a long lineage of astronomical achievement.

Whenever we actively attempt to change the white supremacist narrative that they are great for no other reason other than the color of their skin, it is met with controversy. When we challenge this idea of subcategorical social Darwinism, we are made to look inferior or as reverse racists. We must begin to realize that we come from a great people and that we've been doing more things than dominant society is willing to give us credit for.

However, when credit is given to us, an asterisk always follows it. Affirmative action, minority scholarships, and political correctness are always the headlines. Again, while memory is critical, these social systematic initiatives don't give us a leg up against others. It does nothing but provide the opportunity for people such as Cornel West, LeBron James, Ben Carson, and many others to have a shot at exhibiting their skills and abilities in a wider global kaleidoscope.

We can't get caught in these petty racial and patriotism games. Being cognizant of these experiences isn't anti-white, black, brown, red, or yellow, and it doesn't make you divisive of the United States. Instead, it makes you pro-human. The truth can be discomforting, but it must be told so that when we tell our children about these stones, they will understand the significance of their purpose in the collective imagination.

When our children are confronted with a culture that thinks less of them, even before they can speak, they will know to take these stones with them to help them navigate those hindrances of mazes that they will encounter. That memory of preexisting greatness can be used as a countervailing weapon to counterattack obstacles on their road toward success.

Also, we can't romanticize just our greatness; we must also not forget the struggle as well. We can't be absent-minded about the institutionalized discrimination and racism that still exists. We have many who are still struggling and fighting for equal seats at the dominant society's table and for the ability to create their own.

We don't want to create a dichotomy of black elitism and underrepresented blacks. We must all stand as one. We can't be ashamed to know that our grandmothers slaved away in someone's kitchen or that our father was some white family's driver. We must understand the struggle that occurred so that we can enjoy some of the limited privileges that we benefit from today. Those people were looked at as even less than we are today. Once we remember that, then we won't be so stuck-up on ourselves.

We must resurrect the memory that has been stolen and bastardized because we have a responsibility to control the narrative of our story. If we lose control of the narrative, other people who come along probably won't tell the story from a factual point of reference that disputes the whitewashed narrative they try to attribute to us. It is up to us to protect our memory and take those stones to create monuments.

Our job is to provide to those coming behind a biography of where they came from, why they are here, and how they can achieve. We must not challenge the verdict of suffering with retrials, but we must fight against those cases against us from the historical context of landmark victories and achievements that are in our collective memory.

CHAPTER 4

WHITEWASHING

Michelangelo's infamous, or famous (depending on whom you ask) portrait of the Last Supper has been met with praise and scrutiny. The painting displays a white version of Jesus and the twelve disciples, which many people look at as the standard of Christianity in a global perspective. Studies show that a form of Christianity was prevalent in Egypt in the period of 1 AD and stretched to Carthage about a century later.

The whitewashing of black existence and cultural experience is ever rampant today in a society that uses customs of different groups for profit, in what many scholars define as cultural appropriation—even though the United States prides itself on being defined as a giant melting pot, due to the multiple number of ethnicities that constitute its population.

However, cultural appropriation is a little different. In most instances it occurs when members of a dominant culture exploit the customs, trends, or doings of a lesser group without having a concise understanding of the history or tradition.

Almost all groups outside of the white race fall victim to having their customs borrowed or in some occurrences stolen. As previously stated in the opening paragraph Christianity was outright stolen and flipped to support the ideals of Europeans. Blacks now are feeling the brunt of their culture, traditions, and doings, going through the motions of being appropriated for commodification. We see this mainly in fashion, music, and black vernacular.

In the music industry, it has been going on as early as the fifties. Some scholars can even predate it to earlier periods. Many white artists would borrow the stylistic aesthetic of black artists who had their music silenced to mainstream audiences and then would perpetuate the notion that they created it. You can see this in the rock 'n' roll genre by Elvis Presley and slowly with rhythm and blues today with the likes of Sam Smith.

While records labels are ushering major singers into making more club/rap-oriented music, a new genre is starting to take over the musical atmosphere known as blue-eyed soul. We can't assume or have the belief that blacks should own a copyright over this type of music, but artists such as Anthony Hamilton, Musiq Soulchild, and others have been pushed to backdrops of the spotlight to escort in the ilk of Justin Timberlake and Robin Thicke. That is the quintessential example of disdain that most people have: blacks are denied the ability to obtain the same level of profit margins that white artists are allotted. While white singers are given the opportunity to flourish in multiple facades of musical expression, blacks who want any type of mainstream exposure are walked through a narrow, musical, unilateral hallway.

Just recently at the 2014 Grammys, the world was allowed to bear witness to what many argued was a form of cultural appropriation when the award for best rap album was presented. Many people in hip-hop circles were hailing Kendrick Lamar's debut Good Kid M.A.A.D. City as one of the greatest debuts from a rap artist ever, but the panel that the Grammys enlisted thought differently when they gave the award to the white artist Macklemore. Even though Macklemore rode on the success of Thrift Shop and the gay acceptance song of "Same Love," many still didn't feel that the award was his. This just reinforces the legacy of black genius, which fails to be acknowledged in the larger global atmosphere.

Kendrick Lamar that night was subsequently turned into my generation's Chuck Berry, Little Richard, Diana Ross, New Edition, Tupac, and countless others. A gold-plated award isn't the root of the disdain that many black artists and listeners have. Instead, it's the reminder of how we are viewed. Even though black musical selections project a wide array of emotions, these artists amplify the deepest thoughts and silent voices of Africans whose aspirations and dreams were diminished and reduced to nothing but mere tools. These artists were singing about deep romance, their place in the United States, and the love they had for one another, even though they had every reason to believe they had nothing to live for. Even though many artists weren't allowed to get a pinch of commercial success until the sixties or even have their videos played on TV (MTV) until Michael Jackson, we still rose to be some of the greatest musical iconographic figures in today's climate, which includes the likes of Beyoncé, Jay-Z, Kanye West, Usher, and others. Yet with these well-respected and talented artists, we are still reminded through the memory of Nas, Kendrick Lamar, Snoop Dogg, Mos Def, and a multitude of others that black genius isn't always respected outside of our communities, unless someone from a dominant culture appropriates the sound to tailor to that person's own group.

Rap/hip-hop isn't well respected anyway unless it's fashioned in such a way that appeases the safeness of the dominant society—which, however, is oxymoronic to its origins. Hip-hop culture has always been defiant and an outlet for rebellious individuals to go against the grain of prominent society. Even the fashion in hip-hop is edgy and different from the norm; even institutions such as the NBA implemented dress codes to try to push the image away from their brand. Most people categorize that as the Allen Iverson rule.

Eurocentric models of dress have established a universal standard; everything that counteracts or goes against them are looked down upon, either as being inferior or inadequate. So when anyone, especially someone of a marginalized culture, goes against the norm, that person's dress is almost immediately ghettoized. Even when we wear items that were designed by white stylists and add our individual flare, the clothing becomes devalued.

Hoodies, gold chains, tilted hats, logo tees, and a multitude of other "street wear" are looked down upon, unless dominant society appropriates it for events such as Halloween. Even though they are capitalizing off our dress for profit, we are still looked at as a joke at the end of the day. The issue at hand isn't that our style of dress isn't perceived in favorable manners in matters of taste, but the underlying prejudices and subjugations that come with it. It's not the dress that most people have an issue with, but the person that clothing is covering.

Even though cultural clothing trends are ever evolving and are not necessarily the same from coast to coast, many blacks who adhere to these cultural stylistic aesthetics experience the same type of treatment. They are still followed in stores, their intelligence is still questioned, and people still experience Negro-phobia.

In essence the clothing culture appropriation is merely dominant culture using indigenous dress without respect for its context and also for monolithic profit for their society. For instance, when you see do-rags or head scarves—sleepwear to keep coarse hair intact—being marketed as everyday dress items, know that it is being bastardized for reasons outside its original context or use. Also, when we look at the rigid dichotomy between dress and language, we somehow notice how members outside certain marginalized groups subconsciously associate one with the other.

When you see white people dress up as rappers or gang members for Halloween, as if they are making a cheap attempt to act out a contemporary minstrel show, notice the hand gestures and how their vernacular switches. Even though black vernacular or African American Vernacular English (AAVE) has its own set of rules, it's always interpreted as an infantile, ghettoized, and broken form of language. That's why I always find it humorous when you see others outside black capacities saying things like, "Yo yo yo, nawl what I mean," whenever they are dressed in black costume, it's basically as if they are alluding to their underlying views of how they perceive us to be. Describing AAVE can't be explained in a single essay, but a few of the main rules are the phonology, the distinctive vocabulary that it possesses, the use of double negatives, and the dropped copula of "be." Ironically, it's wrong in black culture but is globally accepted in Arabic, Russian, and Hebrew speech. So when I see people in black costumes, I almost always downgrade it because they've studied the dress, but fail miserably at emulating the verbiage. Even now in this modern day of social media, you can see companies hiring young hipsters to run their pages and to post on their behalf, using modern slang that sometimes doesn't fit the setting it is normally used for. For example, I recall IHop using the term "on fleek" to describe their pancakes. Even though in a literal sense it may sound correct, "on fleek" is usually reserved for human stylistic characteristics.

Many minority groups don't have issue with slang being borrowed by others who fall outside the cultural or racial lines, but in most instances it's always used for political, capitalistic, or degrading connotations. This past election season (November 2014), you could see Democratic Governor candidate (Texas) Wendy Davis wearing a Wu-Tang sweatshirt. By all means she may be a fan, but with the nature of its release, it seemed like a last-minute ploy to get young people to the polls for their votes. Most people won't vote for you because you connect or attempt to associate with hip-hop, because they are probably more politically conscious than people give them credit for.

Caring about our culture and being compassionate about the manner in which it is represented by outsiders is in no way trying to repudiate white existence, because that would be counterproductive to the ultimate goal of having difference without hierarchy. The United States is looked at as being an accumulation of diverse cultures and ethnicities.

So, in a country that has demonized, degraded, and humiliated minority experience, this is not meant to be an essay or a piece telling white people or any other sect that they shouldn't enjoy black cultures or any culture that falls outside its proximate paradigm. I'm asking them only to question the reasoning behind appropriating others' cultures for jokes or capitalistic intentions.

CHAPTER 5

DEAR YOUNG REAL NIGGA

Dear Young "Real Nigga,"

I see you "thugging" now. However, I remember when you wore light-up cartoon shoes, but I guess you had to grow up.

When I look at you, at age sixteen, I see a spitting image of me. We are both from the hood, but at this point we are still not from the hood. Due to the circumstances of us being at the poverty line, having a single mother, and having no direction where we want our life to begin, let alone end, society has given us the stereotypical right to be criminals, to have absent fathers and single black mothers, and to create other circumstances that trouble our environments.

As a teenager who has no idea what he wants to do in life, being surrounded by people either dying or going to jail is the welcome gate to hell. I understand blacks are always in competition with each other about something. No one wants to be "dusty." I can't lie, $5.25 (minimum wage was $5.15 when I was seventeen) couldn't put Jordans on my feet. I don't want you to be a man who sells his soul or compromises what is right over a pair of sneakers. There was a point in my reality where I thought you either did drugs or sold them.

My uncles told me about a time when the hood was just financially poor, but now our mental mind frames are in poor states. I'm not here to force you to be something. I want you to understand that your options do include gangbanging or drug dealing or both. I just don't want you to be ignorant to the fact that college is an option; trade school, hell, even an average job is possible. I understand "hoes" come when you're chasing dollars. These other "real niggaz" are only selling you a dream. Yeah, they are sexing many chicks, but do you honestly think they settled down? No, like one of my uncles, they grow to be men with matching shirt/short fits, a backward hat, talking about what they used to do and the hoes they used to screw. You should want more than that. Find someone you can marry. If you feel having a slew of hoes promotes masculinity, then you are just another male who is plain clueless. As a man you will know that pussy is pussy, and you should never fall in love with it, but fall in love with the intangibles she possesses. How much pussy you obtain doesn't make you real. Being real comes from your mind frame.

Being real means consistently standing up for what you believe in, instead of what's popular. Being a criminal just gives the police a reason to arrest you and a judge merit to sentence you. But being a man who stands up for what is right, using intellect and intelligence, makes you dangerous to the opposition. Not only are you bringing attention to issues, but you are also probably motivating others to open their blind eyes to see what's really going on.

You need to realize, young man, before the transatlantic slave trade, we come from a rich history of kings and queens. We were raped of our heritage and forced to conform to what whites wanted. Our men were beaten and forced to work miserable lives. If you won't do it for yourself, at least do it for those men whose freedom was suspended, because that slave blood is running through you. You owe it to those ancestors to make something of yourself, more than just another number in a prison or another dead man that a preacher has to lie about at a funeral.

I'm not preaching to you like I'm a saint because it took me until the age of twenty before I knew better, but it's my moral obligation to motivate you to do better. Because besides the money, women, and attention, thugging isn't you.

So how about you calm down? Yeah, you'll lose a lot of women, the quantity will fall, but the quality will make up for it. The money won't come as quickly, but the efficiency it comes in will make up for it. Most importantly, the respect you will receive will last for generations. Remember, it's cool to be smart because at the end of the day, thugs don't retire well.

You may not hear this often, but I love you, and I want you to succeed in this game of life.

CHAPTER 6

FREE LARRY HOOVER

Larry Hoover. Many may only know him because of Rick Ross. Well, he was more than just a line in a hook of the song. He was the leader, head honcho, commander in chief of one of the largest black street gangs in the United States, the Gangster Disciples.

If you are familiar with either Chief Keef or the drill music movement, then you have a clear inclination of what these new age street rap artists from Chicago represent. They constitute the problem of the adolescent black-on-black genocide that is plaguing the inner city of Chicago's West and South Side (other places also). However, claiming that gang affiliation is the root of problems that persist in these inner socially deprived cities of collapse perpetuates us to ignore the political, economic, educational, and social disenfranchisement. Black-on-black crime is just a branch of the issues that factor into the decrepit and deprived communities that many of these gang members reside in.

On the surface level, it seems that black-on-black violence is the root of the problem instead of a separate branch of the root. While it would be intellectually disingenuous to blame a black community for every drug sale, overdose, or murder that occurs, it is worthy of cogitation when we examine the influx of violence that occurs. Chicago isn't an exceptional community because we can find Chicagos in every corner of the world, not just in the United States. For the sake of this piece, Chicago is important because of the gang culture that exists.

It's important to note that organized crime didn't start with black gangs. Instead, we can point to the Irish, Polish, and Italian gangs that preceded the Vicelords, Blackstones, and Gangster Disciples. Black street gangs started off solely as groups of young black individuals forming social coalitions. These proceeded to become coalitions that lived to protect their neighborhood turf from opposing groups that occupied other neighborhoods. Just like any other corporation or nonprofit organization, making money is always a primary goal. While my argument isn't based on what causes youth to join gangs, my argument is the absence of elder leadership for these gangs. You could hear a proliferation of males saying, "On King David," and "On King Larry," as they spoke with the individuals around them. As a child I paid no mind to it, mainly because as a youth my knowledge of the inner workings of black street gangs was diluted with the perception generated by the media.

I remember one time I was attending the Taste of Chicago as a youth. This event was one of the highlights of my annual summer trips when I visited family in Gary, Indiana. My uncle took my cousin and me there to enjoy the daily festivities. I have several people who are close to me who happen to be involved or who have had prior affiliations with different sects of the Gangster Disciples, so I was able to point out quite a few members solely off tattoos and other branding signs that were displayed on some of the people I came across. The people who were symbolically paying homage to David Barksdale and Larry Hoover most likely never met either of the two, since Larry Hoover was sent to prison in 1997 and David Barksdale was murdered in 1974. However, these two garnered respect not only from their gangster constitutes, but also from those outside that capacity. Respect can be gained in three ways: love, money, fear, or some combination of the three. Larry Hoover was a commander to these disciples who followed behind his leadership. I'm not here to convince others to search for the good in Hoover, but his influence is worthy of cogitation. He sold a dream that some may consider a nightmare to not only youth, but also other adults within his community. Yes, we are aware that Hoover sold and distributed his drugs. We can acknowledge that he contributed in the poisoning of his people. He played crucial roles in murders and robberies, but that's not why he is needed. Larry Hoover in the physical isn't needed, but that influential charismatic appeal is needed now, more than ever. Everyone is looking for someone to be the next king, just as those in the hood are looking for Larry Hoover to be free.

I'm not here to argue that Larry Hoover was a great moral agent of positive change, but like Dr. Martin Luther King Jr., he provided a dream to troubled youth that someone like King was there, and many of them bought it. Even though girls are not dismissed from being involved in gang activities, the large demographic that makes up black street gangs is young black males. Many black males associated with these organized crime groups come from homes where the father is absent, the community is flooded with drugs, extreme cases of unemployment are present, and guidance is missing. "What would Dr. King do?" is a usual phrase that you may hear from elders or people who don't have direct relations with these communities. However, Dr. King, unlike many of our present leadership, would be on the ground identifying with those he was trying to help. I'm saying that other community leaders are absent from the locations they are trying to serve, but King is seen as an iconographic figure because many of those deprived that he fought for felt they could touch him in a hyperbolic sense. Even though Dr. King didn't do any direct work with the Gangster Disciples, he did live in an apartment in Chicago that was located in the Vicelords' neighborhood territory. Even though this may not seem like anything major for improving the disenfranchisement they were experiencing, it did, however, show that someone iconic like Martin Luther King Jr. cared. If you truly want to be a leader for your people, it is imperative to be in the community with your people.

Larry Hoover was half of who King was. He was very visible in these communities, even while being incarcerated, but he lacked the moral consistency and the commitment to upliftment that King exhibited. Law enforcement and many outside his faux jurisdiction look at Hoover as problematic, but the citizens who claim that black flag see Larry as a savior and royalty. Dr. King not only fought for the end to racial hatred, but he was also prominent in the fight for jobs, opportunity, and income equality. If you are unable to feed the people, then you are unqualified to lead the people. Organizations such as the Southern Christian Leadership Conference are in part like the Gangster Disciples because they can't exist without revenue. During Hoover's reign the Disciples had a horizontal type of sociological leadership. We attempt to provide youth from impoverished communities examples of what they can achieve, but those examples don't provide any tangible economical resources.

Hoover helped lead a criminal entity that provided jobs. Even though those employment opportunities were illegal, it still put currency in the pockets of the gang members. Dollars at the end of the day can even make criminal activities make sense. Leaders who are trying to deter gang activity must always keep in mind the importance of generating revenue. Even though these gangs generate revenue through illicit means, Hoover provided people a sense of agency. Even though the current media paints King with the brush of an iconographic lovable figure, many people, including blacks, disapproved of what King was doing. He was criticized for going against the white establishment, while Hoover was criticized for a different reason. Hoover was criticized for wreaking havoc within the community that many cherished.

Larry Hoover once tried to market the GDs as an organization that stood for Growth and Development (a nonprofit charity), but it was still being used as a criminal enterprise to launder money, move drugs, and perform other illicit means to generate revenue. Even though Larry Hoover wasn't as rich as many think, he projected this image due to the material things he flaunted.

In many of these communities that idolized Hoover, the residents live in places where poverty is looked at as normal, instead of realizing that the class above poverty is what Americans consider normal. Even though the term middle class is considered an ambiguous term, the term is where most feel they fall because it separates them from poverty or the cusp of it. Hoover and other high-ranking officials gave people the concept that they could floss and shine as well. Having a home, car, and disposable income is normal to most Americans, but in eviscerated urban areas, these things make individuals Godlike. Picket fences and green grass are foreign to many of Hoover's followers, but he provided a sense of hope that it was achievable. Just how King emulated and Malcolm taught us that education was the passport to the future, Hoover propelled the notion that carrying a black flag was the ticket to the promised land. Hoover is needed just as King was, even though their goals were not the same.

We have adults who try to get children to defer from the thug lifestyle instead of trying to understand it. I frequently hear Dr. Michael Eric Dyson telling adults that before we tell children to lift up their pants, we must first lift their dreams and their expectations. We won't corrode the problems in the hood until we hear and feel where the hood is coming from. Hoover was esoteric in his relationship with the community. He understood the struggle, and he made a conscious effort to alleviate himself from it. Others followed in his steps. Like King, Hoover was recalcitrant in following the orders of a higher authority. Even though that defiance led to his ultimate demise as a street leader, that same defiance is what propelled him as a street legend. We have to respect his intransigent attitude, but as people who want to better the community, we must figure out ways to circumvent his practices into mechanisms that are not just legal, but that are apparatuses that promote ownership. If you don't own your gifts or the movement by financial means, then you just end being a high-paid slave to someone else.

King provided a dream, and Hoover provided hope for those who were in despair. Hoover could have been more. He was Malcolm Little before he found the X. Hoover till this day still has the youth on lock, even while he's locked down. There are thousands of Larry Hoovers that exist to this day, but they aren't using their leadership for the upliftment of a people. Instead, their leadership is keeping their neighborhoods impoverished in the department of hope. If Larry Hoover told the hood to clean up the sidewalk, they would do it just out of respect for him. If he told them to build legitimate industries to employ members of the hood, they would.

The kids followed Hoover because he was visible, he had material wealth, and he didn't bow down in the face of adversity. He provided uncompromising leadership that's missing from a lot of the figures who speak for the community today. These etic views of how to change our communities can't compare to the emic ones because they are ultimately the ones who have to live through the decisions that are cast upon them from outsiders. The apotheosis of Larry Hoover's reign was a bittersweet one. A man who had so much power couldn't live up to the King legacy that the streets bestowed upon his head. Now we must realize that our kids don't need a singular figure like King or Hoover, but they just need to see the ideals and leadership of those two resonate in everyday people who want the best for the community.

A lot of these kids aren't really bad; they are just following what they see, because no one is around to lead them. Either gang leaders who once kept their gangs moving like an organized crime mob are incarcerated, or they're strung out on drugs. You can lead the children by simply being a local sports coach, a father, or anyone who can relate to their day-to-day struggle, but still offers symbols of hope.

We don't want to free Larry Hoover, the partial influence of this gang culture, but we need that spirit to motivate these youth to want more and to be better. That person doesn't have to be Larry Hoover. Frankly, I don't want it to be him, but young black men need someone to follow. Instead, we are trying to piece together why they are targets. Whether you are looked at as Raymond Washington, Larry Hoover, Tookie Williams, Guy Fisher, Willie Lloyd, or G-Chain, just note that someone is watching you.

The greatest teachers are the ones who profess lessons that can't be spoken, only watched.

CHAPTER 7

NOBODY DID IT LIKE MEECH

*To be honest, because evidently they didn't like what I was doing, or
what they thought I was doing. That's how I look at it. Anytime
you're Black and you got a little power, and you're trying to be successful and you've got money, just for some reason then here they come.*

—*Big Meech*

Blacks will not, refuse to, and are inept to stick together. Is this just a stereo-
type, or is it a truth that others accept, including us? Of course we can
come together to party, tweet about award shows, and argue about who's
the best emcee—Jay-Z, Weezy, or Nas—but what about coming together to
build the straggling black economy?

Love, respect, and trust are hard to come by. Without it, can you honestly
say you can build something sustainable? Of course you've heard of Black
Wall Street, but one organization in particular exemplified how far love, respect, and trust can get you into creating a multimillion-dollar empire. If you
haven't guessed by now, that was B.M.F.—Black Mafia Family.

I'm almost certain that most people think it's absurd to channel Big
Meech and the Black Mafia Family as a way to unite the black community to
achieve economic prosperity, but take the drug element out and universally

substitute it with something else, and you will be surprised how effective their formula can be.

Meech and B.M.F.'s main goal was to get money and upgrade their lives and the economic condition of their loved ones. Contrary to what some Fox News watchers may believe, no one wants to live and die poor or raise terror among their community just for thrills. Everyone wants and deserves to have a chance living life to its maximum fulfillment. What Meech did consisted of providing an opportunity for people who under most circumstances were trained to hate and despise one another. He had Crips, Bloods, Vicelords, Gangster Disciples and others working together to accomplish a common goal: making money and improving living conditions.

I'm certain that the majority of blacks are not gang members, but when it comes to unity, why can't we ask, "Why can't it be?"

Why can't blacks dominate the black hair and hair-care industry, for example? Why can't a group come together instead of allowing Asians to pimp us by selling products that are solely for our usage, instead of keeping those dollars circulating in the black community?

Again, we know essentially that Big Meech was a high-level drug dealer, but when you dig deeper, you'll figure out that he used business-type principles to build a corporation-type business that not only motivated workers, but also provided incentives to excel beyond just "getting by." Like those black business owners in Tulsa, Oklahoma, who set up shops in areas of northern Tulsa known as Black Wall Street. They showed what could happen and what the black dollar could amount to. Meech and company showed nationally what could become if blacks came together for a common purpose, and most feel what it did could never be matched.

When you hear or see Free Meech, it's not the drug lord or accused murderer (never convicted or went to trial), but the Meech business model that incorporated trust, love, and respect for a common goal. Condoning drugs that dissipate people's lives is never the way to go, but if you can substitute drugs with something legal and fulfilling to build positivity within a community, then the heavens are the limit. That black dollar can grow and flip itself continuously throughout our hands countless times and help perform positivity growth if we all can just love, trust, and respect one another enough to come together for that common goal.

Black people have a powerful weapon of mass destruction in their position, but for some reason they refuse to use it. We have nearly a trillion dollars' worth of spending power at our disposal. A Neilsen study produced an article highlighting black spending habits: "Currently 43 million strong, African-American consumers have unique behaviors from the total market. For example, they're more aggressive consumers of media and they shop more frequently. Blacks watch more television (37%), make more shopping trips (eight), purchase more ethnic beauty and grooming products (nine times more), read more financial magazines (28%) and spend more than twice the time at personal hosted websites than any other group (**www.neilsen.com**)." Instead of attempting to circulate that through our community, we choose to focus more on the politics of how we are treated. We feel that our path to the promised land begins and ends with electing people to our legislative bodies. Meech didn't operate that way; he believed in the power of the dollar.

Voting is important, but that's not what is going to get our voices heard. People are allowed to talk bad about us, and we can't do anything about it. You know why? We have no self-induced economic empowerment that they are afraid will hurt them. When someone says something that is anti-Semitic, it is always handled quickly because the Jewish community has an economic power structure.

When black folks collectively get an economic agenda, then they will begin to get a slice of the American pie and not the crumbs that fall to the floor. Time spent building and executing an economic agenda should replace the time we've spent fighting for social inequality. Once others see that we aren't dependent on them, then attitudes are likely to change. Even if attitudes do not change, black people won't have to beg for inclusion. Instead, they will have their own. Black folks seem to have an underlying fear of doing for self to combat the issues that they struggle with daily. Economics will take a group effort as opposed to the social talk that just requires someone to be the loudest. We don't need people to sympathize with us. We must make them respect us as a collective.

We live in a time in which education and trades are more accessible to blacks than they have ever been, but since we live in this utopia of a post-racial society, we don't incorporate the individual talents we all have to strengthen our communities. We have been sucked into this trend of individualism. We are more concerned about our next personal pleasure, instead of finding joy in serving others. Even if you feel you don't have the skills to create other streams of income, you should also keep in mind that we live in the information age.

You can go to Google and learn a multitude of things to help you generate extra income. You can still have a job working for someone else, but you shouldn't be limited to just one stream. Also, we have so many other individuals who have started their own ventures; we shouldn't be afraid to ask questions or advice. We have to stop being scared to step outside our comfort levels. We must spread our eagle wings.

Big Meech created a drug empire by not settling. Let's not commit criminal offenses, but why can't we create taxi companies, law firms, clinics, consulting companies, and franchises in our own community? If you connect with the people, they will follow. We have enough workshops and town hall meetings addressing concerns in our communities. Now we must take what we've learned and apply it to eliminate the struggle we live with. Meech lived a life that many from socially neglected areas wanted, and they followed his philosophy. They understood that they may not get the largest slice of pie, but they would get a piece and wouldn't have to settle for crumbs that were left over.

We have to practice what we preach to our people. A lot of us have degrees that are just a piece of paper we do nothing with. You can use your education as a means to justify your rants on the issues facing black folks in the United States, or you can use the education you received to lift up those who may never ever have an access to that education. Education is not just limited to an institution of higher learning, but if you have knowledge in a particular realm, exchange it with your other comrades. Reach one, teach one!

Free Big Meech, not the drug dealer, but men who represent the art of helping others and employing them. We need more enterprises that create owners and not educated workers. We won't see the fruits of our labor if we do not yield those crops on our own farms.

CHAPTER 8

THE INDICTMENT OF BLACK INTELLIGENCE

In 1619 twenty indentured servants were brought to Jamestown, Maryland, from Africa in a Dutch ship. From this moment on, black people (even brown people) have been arguing their case against the indictment of black intelligence in the court of white privilege. These attitudes against those with darker skin are the basis of Western bigotry and racism.

When a delegation of resources is allocated toward one racial sector of society by the means of commodification of humans, this sets the foundation for not only racial formation, but also psychological attitudes of intellectual inferiority of one group against another. With these types of implications, black people are made to believe they don't have souls, nor do they have the rights of practical humanity like everyone else. Black folks were first treated like animals, the types of animals that are considered cattle. We were stolen, bought, and resold with no regards.

When we are made to believe that our brains are not designed in the manner that GOD designed everyone else's, we are psychologically being murdered in the form of modern-day intellectual lynchings. We can be portrayed as coons on television, exploited for our culture to earn commercial profit for others, but then they arraign us in the court of public opinion as thugs because we may listen to some hip-hop. Since that is characteristic of thuggery, how can the United States explain a democracy that denied black men the right to vote? And once they started winning elections, they took it away in the means of poll taxes, threats, and literacy tests that most of them couldn't even pass. Let's not also forget the women who waited even longer to be recognized as people worthy to cast a ballot. If that's not gangster, I don't know what is. This type of skepticism of our humanity keeps us suspected of doing something wrong, even when we may be right.

This allows us to be victimized like Richard Sherman after his lively post-game interview in the 2014 NFC Championship game. Whether or not that tirade was designed to be a marketing ploy to market his brand, we must at least acknowledge the discussion that arose from it. The word *thug* now has become a euphemism for a modern-day connotation for the term nigger. Due to new methods of what I like to call "modern-day racism," people will try to deflect their racist views on these sorts of instances by reflecting on historical examples of people who were deemed thugs so they appear not to have these racist attitudes. They might reference John Gotti, Jesse James, or anyone who isn't a current figure today. This is important because when you look at how the word *thug* is used today, it only seems to be applicable to black people, black males especially.

Back to the case of Richard Sherman. When he gets indicted as a thug, this now has black people beginning to criminalize our own people. We talk about him graduating with a 4.2 from high school, a 3.9 from Stanford, and beginning a master's program in his final year of eligibility, all while playing football. It's almost oxymoronic for someone from Compton to have these types of accomplishments, at least in the eyes of the dominant society. Since he is breaking down jock stereotypes, we forget to identify the root of the issue. Now we must ask ourselves: how will Jamal from Brooklyn who graduated high school with a 2.5, attended a local community college, and works as a janitor be perceived? I have zero issue with Sherman's actions, but when we only highlight these exceptional individuals, we at times disconnect them from the rest in our communities, who may fall outside of that pale. White America starts to look at these people as exceptional Negroes and not like the rest of those niggers. These differences allow us to be treated differently in the eyes of those from the governing society.

For instance, when Justin Bieber was having issues concerning DUIs, allegedly spitting on fans, drag racing, flipping off the paparazzi, and other deviant behavior, there are specials on not just networks like E, but on the news networks too, trying to get to the root of why the United States' precious child was having behavioral issues. They say maybe it's the hip-hop crowd he's hanging around, the absence of a childhood that was taken away from him at a young age, or maybe a result of his superiority over the adults who cater to him. Maybe due to the power imbalance of a child over an adult, they are subject to an inferiority complex that develops into a psychological issue, putting them in a position where they can't say, "No, Justin." But when Todd Bridges and others of his ilk are in these same positions, they are just looked at as drug addicts and thugs. Some will argue that they are looking at us through science, but looking at statistics doesn't give you the bigger picture. You can't judge groups of people unless they are given an equal playing field. Most are not judging us through equal lenses, but through their race, class, and even their bigotry.

When black's intelligence and humanity are not treated with fairness, we are put in a position where we are consistently begging for equality. The problem with this is that change will not happen unless we demand it. Black brothers and sisters are only begging, we aren't demanding it. Marches, panels, and performing research activism is one thing, but changing public policy is more effective. We as a people must demand that the state legislators we vote for not only take our vote, but also work for our vote. The black vote is now being looked at as an automatic Democratic vote, not something that must be earned. Votes should be earned, not given, and black folks haven't been making politicians earn them. Issues in our communities regarding education funding, the prison industrial complex, social services, housing, and more need to be addressed now, and we must demand that they fix these problems now! Since they have our vote, we must make them stand and fight for us in the same manner that we are fighting the effects of white supremacy views on our intelligence and humanity every day.

CHAPTER 9

BLACK GUILT

On May 20, 2015, Kerrie Orozco was killed in the line of duty while attempting to serve felony warrant papers to Marcus Wheeler in Omaha, Nebraska. Marcus also died from the shootout that eventually ensued from their encounter. This incident was heightened to astronomical proportions not because an officer lost her life, but because police brutality has been a hot topic in the US consciousness since the death of Michael Brown in Ferguson.

The narrative has been on the militarization of the police and the manner in which many believe that black people are targeted. Often black victims are criminalized immediately after, so that the public can be provided with justification on why the officer shot or used excessive force. Often black victims have to represent a respectable narrative so they can obtain sympathy and empathy from the public. However, Marcus didn't exhibit any of that. The media immediately reported his rap sheet, even weeks after Officer Orozco was buried. The narrative of "police lives matter" was subliminally juxtaposed with the contemporary slogan of "Black Lives Matter."

This not only reinforces beliefs that the majority culture has, but it also provides many blacks an ambivalent feeling about the roles of police in deprived minority communities. It makes us think that we need tougher police to protect the community and to rid the neighborhood of troublemakers. In a sense these incidents and subsequent violent atrocities against police officers provide reason for them to criminalize, profile, and judge black individuals. Even though black people are attacked by police officers at higher rates than the inverse, these incidents against police are more highly publicized. Officer Orozco was advertised as a staple in the community in which she patrolled. She spoke at after-school centers and coached Little League baseball. In a sense reporters wanted it to be known that she cared for the community and was loved by it. I don't want to argue that this could be defined as philanthocracy, but police as a whole don't have trust within these communities.

As a black male, I feel uneasy and uncomfortable around police, even when I know I've done nothing wrong to warrant these feelings or emotions. Just the sheer fact that I could be stopped or arrested on an erroneous charge forces me to keep my distance from law enforcement. When this story broke, I witnessed a storm of not only white people, but also black people in large numbers asserting that they stood with blue, and that police lives matters. Even though many of the people who stood with the police and the slain officer were black, we began to notice the dichotomy of respectable blacks and "thugs." I am someone who doesn't endorse the current manner in which police departments operate and are institutionalized around the country, but I can, however, embrace the humanity of people dying in an unjust manner. Police are frequently given the benefit of the doubt, even when they are caught on camera abusing citizens. We saw this with Eric Garner. Even though the chokehold was deemed illegal and the coroner ruled it a homicide, the police made the public believe that he died due to his asthma. The salient proverbial fraternal shield that encompasses the police force keeps them from talking down or publicly chastising their fellow officers. The black community, however, isn't afforded this same privilege. We are expected to publicly apologize and forgive for the actions inflicted upon others that have the same melanoid features as we do.

Even during the peak of protest that occurred in New York, black people again were expected to respect the lives of Officers Rafael Ramos and Wenjian Liu when they were viciously murdered. Even though protesters weren't obliged by law to rest their protest, they did it without commotion or grievance. Tupac Amaru Shakur once said, "We can't get peace until those boys get a piece too." On the surface one may assume that he's advocating for the attack of white citizens or law enforcement, but when I hear that lyric, I look at it as something deeper than what may appear on the surface level. When one of our daughters, brothers, fathers, mothers, grandparents, or friends are murdered by those sworn by the law, our comfort levels are being dissipated. When we grieve, it is always taken with a grain of salt from those with opposing viewpoints. Our feelings and innate fears are looked at as imaginative and erroneous, but we are expected to show compassion for those who are part of a system that we are infuriated with. In a sense one can say we are experiencing a form of Stockholm syndrome. We figure that maybe if we show compassion for those who have ambivalent opinions about our struggle, then maybe they could understand our strife. However, it doesn't work like that. Oppressive feelings, misery, and destitution don't take a day off, but only with us is it expected when facts begin to reveal that someone in our community may have done something wrong.

In this case of Kerrie Orozco, blacks began to go on an apology tour by condemning the person who was said to have fired the fatal shot that ultimately killed her. The issue is not with people expressing sadness over this killing, but the issue is in regards to the fact that black people felt it was their obligation to paint themselves with a brush of respectability. Many people who mourned for Michael Brown, put up their hoods for Trayvon, and hold their children a bit tighter for Aiyana Stanley-Jones began to smoke the proverbial, "We Are All One" crack pipe. An onslaught of statements began to brew, not only stating that they stood with blue, but also stating that incidents like this give reason for us to be profiled by law enforcement and others outside our community. For my protection as a black child I was taught that if I wanted to gain respect and if I wanted to avoid racial profiling it was necessary to act in a manner that appeased white society.

When we create these faux requirements of black responsibility articulated out of the mouths of those who are covered in blackness, they start off using their credentials of being emically invested within black culture, but these same black people end up taking an quasi etic stance because they aren't advocating for equal treatment that is outside the scope of appealing to white comfort. If safety from police is derived from bowing down and not being intransigent to one's cultural aesthetic in terms of how we dress, speak, and indubitably exist, then that is not liberation, but sanctified oppression to those who feel they are sanctimonious to us. Freedom is inextricably tied to the power of creating one's self-image. We are in a constant war over our blackness. We are always told to tone it down and assimilate into American culture—in other words, we must make white people comfortable.

Professor Jerry Hough of Duke University posted a tirade via the *New York Times* about the self-defeating behaviors of blacks in the United States. He references how Asians were treated in the country and how they were referred to as coloreds. The racism that Asians faced was very prevalent, but is losing one's identity worth acceptance? He talked about how Asians began to adopt more Americanized first names for the children, and they also began to have a proliferation of interracial relationships. Professor Hough correlated this to the teachings of Dr. Martin Luther King by expressing that the Asians followed him, while the blacks chose to follow Malcolm X.

That statement resonates because Malcolm was seen as someone who promoted violence, when in essence he was campaigning for protection. Turning the other cheek wasn't an option for Malcolm. Instead, he wanted to put an end to us getting slapped by those who hated us. Black people are chastised for not being perfect. We are made to believe that those imperfections are the reason why we are targeted by law enforcement. We are made to feel sorry for ourselves because we don't fit the American mold, and we are shamed for empowering ourselves when we attempt to deconstruct the brutality that is inflicted upon us.

Showing empathy for a lost life is not problematic, but when we are asked as a collective to be sorry for the actions of an isolated individual, then that is a problem. It isn't uncommon for law enforcement to come to our communities to tell us that we need to assist in their investigations, but it is rare that a law enforcement officer would even be called to an affluent community to discuss issues that happen there. On June 7, 2015, a video was uploaded showing excessive force against a group of black middle schoolers in McKinney, Texas; but it is very unlikely that a conference will be held to tell them about the dangers of racial profiling. Actions by those who don't wear the cloak of blackness will never be asked to do better, hold one another accountable, or change their myopic views, but we are given that burden to bear.

Malcolm stated that chickens would come home to roost. When you allow citizens to be deprived of their human right to exist, then it shouldn't be shocking once some blowback begins to occur. I will never advocate for unwarranted violence against anyone, even if that person is a cop, but I will advocate for black people not to be sorry for their own oppression that is funded through their own tax dollars.

America, I truly apologize that I am not sorry that I make you uncomfortable.

I'm black first...my sympathies are black, my allegiance is black, my whole objectives are black...I am not interested in being American, because America has never been interested in me.

—Malcolm X

CHAPTER 10

WHO REALLY LOVES OUR BLACK BOYS?

A re black boys the target of a racist society, or are we merely criminalizing them to the point where they're fearful of one another? Who really loves black boys aside from their mother? Have we taken a moment to ask young black boys, "Who really loves you?" Do we lead young black males toward a path that primes them only to see their masculinity as a beginning and end of who they really are? We have been taught through homophobic principles not to show compassion and love for them because that's not masculine; who really cares? How do we end this cycle of autophobia?

We have a generation of black males who walk around with their heads held down, always looking over their shoulder because they may be Zimmerized or shot dead because their music is too loud. We have men walking with their backs slouched, which allows others to ride them and make them feel ashamed of whom they are. When you walk with your back straight, no one can slow you down because you're moving with a purpose. We have a cohort of brown and dark-skinned boys who are afraid, intimidated, and made to feel dishonest about themselves; this begins the process of what Dr. Cornel West likes to call the niggerization of a people. We have become so fearful of ourselves that we are willing to consent to our own domination from street gangs all the way to enlisting into the armed services to kill people who look like us in foreign countries. We are the pawns of social assassination, all while being economically commodified. Black boys have to come to the context of why am I hated, why am I unsafe, and why am I unprotected? What is it about me that strikes fear not only in white folks, but also in my own damn people? Who is there to teach these boys not to accept this and to fight against it? Who actually cares about our black boys and not about if they will be getting a check in return or personal notoriety, who is really standing up to tell the truths of these black boys who have been stigmatized, victimized, and made to believe that they are a nonfactor in the grand scheme of things?

The life of black boys has been made into a mockery, and they are degraded daily, whether it's for their hairstyles, the way they dress, and even the music they listen to. We as a race have contributed to the ways that these boys are being criminalized in this society. We speak on their dreads and tell them to make sure all their tattoos are covered because we don't want them to be suspected or to be offensive toward corporate (white) United StatesAmerica. We complain about their sagging pants, but how often do we raise their expectations of what they can be? We criminalize their dress, but what are they dressing up for? Or more importantly, what are we dressing them up for? It seems that now it is a capital offense to be outside as a young, black male in this country.

It seems that we only care once it too late. We only tell them they are beautiful once their parents and the community are grieving. Our young people need to know other men are pulling their bootstraps up so they can fight for their rights, so we can eliminate the terror from their hearts. Revolution doesn't have to start with a reaction to a tragedy or oppression; you can ignite a revolution by just having a love in your heart for the people. We have groups of men who have made it out of socially neglected areas, but we have forgotten about the ones left behind. It would be idiotic to expect everyone to work for the cause, but we need more men who are willing to bring those degrees back to the hoods they left and uplift these young boys who don't get the love they deserve. Folks get so worried about their careers, promotions, their status, and not making the oligarchs and plutocrats upset that they are afraid to tell the truth, or they begin to take the role of head field slaves. Not all, but some, of the black elite use their status as a means to talk down to others who may not have had the opportunity to get an education, not just at public schools, but at the illustrious private schools from Yale to Tuskegee. We have elites who think they are better than the less fortunate. Too many of us who are college graduates use that piece of paper as means and justification to devalue others of our race to the point where we leave them out of the positions that the Martins, the W.E.B. Duboises, and others were trying to get us out of. Don't let these made-up views of us being the exception dilute the truth.

Once we are afraid to tell the truth, we allow ourselves as adults to remain niggerized so that we remain adapted to injustice, give up, and ignore the indifferences that occur, leaving our boys lost, with no one to aspire to follow. We have somehow adopted this ideology that we have to make it out of the "ghetto" and never look back, but at one time, when we thought of the ghetto, it wasn't anything demeaning or disgraceful. It was where a whole contour of people came together and had love for one another. But now that we are in a time in which the counterrevolution is winning, we try to divide and separate ourselves from one another.

Not to ignore the work that has been done and is being done, but the counterrevolution is winning. They tell us to use our collective vote to elect state legislators who make laws to protect us, but our issues sit outside the given agenda of a conservative who has special interest groups pulling the strings, and left-wing liberals who don't have a spine to walk upright for us. These legislators also have money thrown at them to care about other social issues, resulting in us getting left out. We continue to be made to feel that we are invisible. The youth are not looking for handouts; they are just looking for someone to love them and to tell the truth about the suffering they are enduring. Not to marginalize black boys from other groups (which all are precious), but we as men especially must not be afraid to express our love for them.

Even if we may disagree ideologically about what needs to be done, we must all care. Not about any status, promotion, or recognition, but we must care for the people. The fighting of oppression is not a sprint, but a long-distance race, and the only thing that will get you to that finish line is to have a strong love in your heart for the people. We can spend time blaming single mothers, the prison industrial complex, white folks, educations, economics, but at the end of it all, who really loves these boys besides their mothers? When was the last time you told a black boy you loved him and wanted him to do well? Like Marvin Gaye said in the summer of 1971, "Save the babies."

Who really cares? If you won't tell them, I am willing to be stripped of my "masculinity" to express to those boys that I love them.

CHAPTER 11

A Letter to My Brother

Behold, how good and how pleasant it is for brethren
to dwell together in unity!
Psalms 133

One of my greatest accomplishments that I am honored to have is the ability to call you, Darius L. Malone, my brother.

During the beginning of Black History Month this year, we began to alternate days sending each other quotes from black figures. Even after Black History Month, we still keep it up, using daily quotes from the likes of W.E.B. to even the rapper YG. They are always appreciated and relevant to things that are poignant to what is happening in my life and things nationally. The words of others are great, but what's more worthy of cogitation is the listening ear you provide and the compassion from your heart that you have not only for others, but also for me when I am down and out. No matter whether I'm upset about a national tragedy or something concerning my personal life at work or in relationships, you've never screened one call or been a moratorium to my issues. You have this keen amicable ability to make the conundrums that I present you a little less stressful. You've probably saved me from a proliferation of gray hair and an early heart attack.

I know you think I'm being mendacious or making an erroneous statement when I place you in my top five influences behind Professor Margaret (Peggy) Jones, Dr. Michael Eric Dyson, Malcolm X, and Martin Luther King Jr., but you're a role model whether you want to believe it or not. You're dialectically and linguistically sound, you possess a sartorial genius that is impeccable, and you are intransigent in your belief that satisfaction leads to complacency and that mediocrity shouldn't be celebrated, nor is black excellence impressive, it is expected! I haven't reached one-quarter of the heights I've dreamed of, but knowing you has provided someone like me (you were told I was typical Omaha nigga…ha-ha) a different narrative to what was possible. I wish to be akin to half the man you are now and to possess an ounce of your moral virtue. You've taught me that getting out of the hood isn't admirable, but it's honorable to build up your hood. Your tenacity for achievement, even when you are under the direst circumstances, is that of much profundity. You never let your immediate predicaments derail you from your long-term goals, and that keeps me motivated.

You're a true Trojan horse. Initially you're thought to be the ideal gentleman (which is right) because you're a Morehouse man, you speak the King's English to the queen's taste. Your intelligence is beyond measure, but you've never forgotten where you came from, and you still remain that same nigga who grew up across the street from the projects. I won't turn this encomium into a dissertation, but I would like to say that you need to step it up. I only say this because you edified me on the words of my now brother from the east, who said, "Whatever you do, strive to do it so well that no man living and no man dead and no man yet to be born could do it any better."

If others knew you like I do, then they would understand that you aren't satisfied being on any list that puts you at any other position aside from No. 1. I have the utmost belief that not only will you climb to No. 1 on my list, but you will be an inspiration to others who are living and those yet to be born. I wish you another year of stunting and flossing. Agape, my negus!

CHAPTER 12

I Wanna Be Like Mike

Growing up, we all wanted to be like Mike—whether it was Jordan, Tyson, or Jackson. Growing in the hood, it was perspicuously given that illicit activity, music, and sports were the only things that gave us a legitimate shot at making it out of our conditions.

Illicit activities usually came with hefty price tags that included damaged ligaments, a prison cell, or an early funeral. Even those risks and the knowledge of those who got caught up in the system never deterred many from choosing that lifestyle because it was either that or starvation. Economic devastation in poor minority communities makes the drug game appealing, while the absence of capital in these same areas stifles opportunities that would provide sustainable chances for these poverty-stricken neighborhoods of economic castration. While you can find more people trying to be music artists and athletes than doctors and lawyers, most still saw it ironically as their lottery ticket out.

It took me twenty years to realize that I also wanted to be like Mike; however, his last name was Dyson. My knowledge of Dr. Michael Eric Dyson happened when he was one of the featured guests on *Hip-Hop Versus America*, a special that was broadcast on Black Entertainment Television. He was very informative but also entertaining as well. His charismatic approach to addressing issues that affect the black community was eye-opening for a college student who was oblivious to the underlying and covert discrimination that people face. Often in poor black communities, the citizens are made to feel as if their predicament is strictly based off them and their lazy attitudes toward hard work. While Dyson doesn't shy away from holding black people responsible, he also isn't afraid to confront the most powerful instead of solely scapegoating the most vulnerable.

That special on BET was a multiple-part feature that displayed other points of view, even though Dyson was the most memorable outside of the rappers that were featured and happened to occupy space in my CD player. His name still resonated in the back of my head, which served a greater purpose once I got to college at the University of Nebraska–Omaha (UNO).

Attending UNO was probably one of the best decisions I've ever made. I say that because it was one class I took that hit me with the greatest force in regards to shaping the man that I am today. During my sophomore year I took a class entitled "Black Women in America," which was taught by one of my greatest influences, Margaret (Peggy) Jones MFA. Even though this class centered around the lives of black women and their erasure from the consciousness of the American psyche, this class inspired me to learn more about blackness and my place not only in the United States, but in the world.

At the age of twenty years old, I was being forced to step outside my epistemological closet of parochialism, and I began to adopt a wider view of what it meant to be black. A couple of months into the course, Professor Jones announced to the class that Dr. Michael Eric Dyson would be delivering the keynote address for the week-long Malcolm X festival that the Black Studies department was hosting. Even though I wasn't too edified on his work, I did however remember him from *Hip-Hop Versus America*, and I was excited to hear him in person.

I mirror my enthusiasm with the excitement of attending a concert of the hottest rapper out; he may not be your favorite, but this type of opportunity is a must. I didn't know what was on me once I entered the College of Public Affairs and Community Service (CPAC) building. Inside, not only did I find Dr. Dyson, but I found a purpose, a career, and a destiny. To hear Dr. Dyson circumvent his lecture around the politics of memory, race, gender, and a multitude of other issues while juxtaposing the works of Greek philosophers such as Aristotle, Plato, and Socrates with the likes of Jay Z, Nas, and Tupac was truly remarkable. At that moment I wanted to be just like him.

As the lecture came to a close, Dr. Dyson set a portion of the night for guests to meet him, so he could sign autographs and take pictures with them. After hearing his speech, I was so in awe that it forced me to step to the back of the line because I didn't know what to say to such an iconographic figure. Once I finally got to where he was seated, the only thing that blurted out of my mouth was, "When is your book about Nas coming?" Instead of asking about public policy, his thoughts on President Obama, a question about Nas came out. He was really cool about that and simply gave the quintessential response that you'd expect from a rapper: "It's coming soon." We took a quick photo, a photo that stills occupies a space in my living room today for guests to see when they visit my home.

Over time I would gather all the writings and books that I could find so that I could consume his genius. Seeing how he spoke and wrote on an array of issues such as the intersectionality of religion, politics, race, and gender was quite interesting because Dyson introduced a wide range of scholars in various fields. But what was more intriguing was his childhood story.

Often we put our idols within an iconographic context, which ends up placing them in a space where their status is unattainable from our own immediate experience. Hearing about his life growing up on the West Side of Detroit and being the son of working-class parents story allowed me to see myself in him. Dyson doesn't shy away from letting folks know he hasn't forgotten his roots or the birthplace of his genius, especially when it's easy for many to assume that this Princeton-groomed intellectual is just another bourgeois professional who has cemented himself within the mainstream and away from the streets. Dyson has shown the importance of infiltrating the professional class while also bridging the gap between the two spaces. He doesn't do it often, but Dyson speaks about his time on the streets in gangs. Even though that isn't a prerequisite to connecting to the streets, it does provide Dyson with the heart to protect, look, and advocate for them.

While I never got caught up in activity like that, I do understand how easy it is to get caught up in your immediate reality while seeing your future through a myopic lens. It's amazing how one individual can single-handedly change the trajectory of one person, even when my encounter with him was on a college campus and on BET. Many from the same communities that I hail from may never step foot on a college campus. It is likely that they will turn on a TV, where his face might be present. That is what makes the genius of Dyson and others of his ilk so special; it is because they meet you where you are and not solely at the place where they want you to be.

When we hear the late Christopher Wallace (The Notorious B.I.G.) rap on the song, "Everyday Struggles," those lyrics speaks on the importance of black leadership acting as a village for the people it claims to protect.

When we hear of a twelve-year-old being one of three suspected in the murder of Jamymell Ray, it makes one wonder where we went wrong. This incident happened in my own city of Omaha. When I see his face, I can see the absence of innocence and a face lacking hope. Instead of initially condemning him, I have to reflect on his image because I not only see other kids I grew up with, but I also see myself. I'm not claiming I was dealt the same cards as the twelve-year-old, whose name is Jarrell Milton, but if I hadn't been afforded mentors who cared for my well-being, then it's probable that I could have faced the same fate that is being brought upon him. A big issue is that we don't internalize these tragedies. Instead, we deflect from them under the notion of, "We aren't like those other niggas."

Many of the posts I've seen directed toward him and children from similar socioeconomic areas speak to broader issues of how adults pathologize them. Instead of embracing and loving them, we vilify them. When you begin to love them, then you can challenge them. Once you love and challenge them, then that opens the door for you to transform them. We can't just damn children without listening to them and being challenged by what they have to say. People need to step outside of these epistemological closets of parochialism and widen their scope so that we aren't talking about another twelve-year-old next week, next month, or a year from now.

How can we expect to change their trajectory in life if we refuse to meet them head on? How can we expect them to accept our challenge for excellence if we condemn them? How can we expect a transformation if we refuse to listen to them so that we can understand them? While it's important to talk about personal accountability, that doesn't allow a pathway for us to ignore systematic and institutionalized factors that reproduce oppression through policies that treat the United States' most vulnerable citizens as a number waiting to get processed instead of humans trying to live. While on the exterior it must seem that they are hateful people, we must keep in mind that these are individuals suffering from traumatic depression who hate the world or who hate their existential reality.

When I read the works or listen to the lectures by Dr. Dyson, he doesn't just reflect the social and institutionalized woes that many are facing like a thermometer. Instead, he acts as a thermostat in how he shapes the way we attack youth violence, poverty, and education, instead of just reflecting issues like a thermometer. Since those issues are intertwined, we must fix those covert issues while we try to diminish the overt problems.

Just as others might want to emulate MJ's fade-away, Tyson's left hook, or Michael Jackson's eloquent moonwalk, I want to exhibit Dyson's articulation of the King's English, his exquisite lexicon, and his uncanny ability to juxtapose Greek philosophy with contemporary black music within a social, political, and educational context. But most importantly I want to match his willingness to uplift the black community.

Dyson not only provides critical commentary and action, but he also gives black men like me a path to a different future that allows them to be successful without selling out to the mainstream at the expense of the underclass.

Everyone isn't going to want to be like Mike, but those children on the corner may want to be like you, and you may be the person that changes their future in the way that Mike did mine.

CHAPTER 13

BLACK EXCEPTIONALISM

Black exceptionalism is a pitfall; black exceptionalism creates space for a few, but excludes many. Exceptionalism is defined as something that is idiosyncratic, unusual, or out of the ordinary.

Within the black community, blacks who fall into the realms of exceptionality are expected to be the next public servants and to be our world's new incoming class of intellectuals. Those who soar above the exceptions of black achievement are heralded to be the next leaders to grab the torch that once gripped the fiery hands of Frederick Douglass, Ida B. Wells-Barnett, W.E.B. Dubois, Mary McLeod Bethune, Martin Luther King Jr., Ella Baker, and many others in the quest to lead blacks to the promised land.

Black exceptionalism has been used as a litmus test for what is wanted for those who fall outside of the capacity of exceptionality. As a child I was always flooded with the notions of making it big in the sports realms, but we have a flurry of black professionals who spoke about how education was the key to making it of a community of destitution. It was always understood that I was to graduate college, get a job, and that I was not to become a statistic.

My friend Darius expressed that while black exceptionalism is the standard we live to aspire to, many in our community still look at it as something that is out of the ordinary. We often hear about black excellence, like it's a surprise, juxtaposed to something that is to be excepted.

We also discussed how black exceptionalism was seen through the myopic lens of whiteness. Black exceptionalism looks at individuals as those who can be perceived as good, or not like the other ones. This gives me flashbacks of my time in predominantly white working and learning environments.

Navigating through the white hegemonic power structure either as a student or an employee has been challenging for me because of the underlying de facto standards that are ever present in a world that has degraded minority experience. Once you enter these spaces, you are between a black culture analysis and white cultural supremacy. When we look at what it means to be American blackness at times is seen as a subcategory, it's a battle of purity versus contamination. Blacks are constantly trying to prove to whites that their image is clean and rid of white-perceived vile connotations.

After I matriculated at the University of Nebraska–Omaha, I took several Black Studies and Sociology courses that started my edification around how overt and institutional racism affects the day-to-day lives of marginalized groups in underlying ways. Aside from the usual cast of black figures and groups such as Martin Luther King Jr., Malcolm X, Booker T. Washington, and the Black Panthers, I began to get introduced to the works of Stokely Carmichael, Marcus Garvey, and Assata Shakur. Upon learning about these newfound exceptional black heroes and heroines, I started to wonder why the history I was given excluded them from the broader consciousness.

Our society is obsessed with comparisons and determining who's the best. Society has even trained us to internalize these differences. Even when we juxtapose Martin with Malcolm, we can see how Martin's character is sensationalized to the point that we glorify his contributions in a way that it is used to vilify what Malcolm stood for. Even though I began to realize that we can love both without condemning the other, I always thought it was suspicious that the historical narrative attempted to force blacks to pick sides. In a sense we were told that if you want to progress in the United States, Martin was the litmus test, while Malcolm sought to extend racial hatred by his "reverse racists" attitudes.

While my love from Martin is always high, my adoration for Malcolm began to flourish. Malcolm reminded me why I idolized Allen Iverson. Iverson's play on the court was exceptional, but he played by his own rules. He wasn't concerned about the mainstream, and he was anti-establishment. Iverson was committed to excellence on the court, but he did it on his own terms. He wore his hair in braids, he had a wide assortment of tattoos, and he indirectly showed kids they didn't have to cater to what white people deemed the standard to be great. His unwillingness to conform probably dilapidated his career, but it impregnated a new idea of what an NBA player looked and played like. Malcolm didn't have King's storied career, but like Garvey, he gave blacks the ideology of self-sufficiency and told us that we can't wait for others to punch our ticket to the promised land. We need to drive ourselves.

As I began to work at my university's library and my local Target, I began to embrace my blackness and to reject standards that probably would have propelled me to promotions. I never broke any rules at my job, but I was never apologetic in my views regarding race and class. Over time my opinions became more vociferous, and I also began to become more expressive in how I talked about issues. Many of my coworkers and superiors began to notice how different I was compared to others; I was always considered someone with extreme potential, but I just didn't know when to shut up. I was always told that they could see me as a preacher, politician, or a lawyer because I talked a lot. As a child (even at times as an adult), I had a shy demeanor and would keep a quiet profile on many things I felt. My mother always raised me to behave, and this almost in a sense took the initiative out of me to challenge things I was ambivalent about.

That was no fault of her own, but black people have been embedded with this notion that we should follow a strict set of the standards that will offer us protection from the power structure by acting in a way that allows us an invitation to their game. This way of thinking is rooted in the realm of respectability politics that have historical connotations that were designed in the hopes it would keep black people safe. Also, I was presented with black male images that were postal points for respectability politics such as Bill Cosby, Ben Carson, and Booker T. Washington.

When I began to get more ingrained into the writings and the lectures of Michael Eric Dyson, I saw that he presented a different image to me. He was black, prominent, educated (PhD from Princeton), intelligent, and unapologetic in his activism for black people. Not only were his writings detrimental to my ideology, but so did the style that he brought while being a surrogate of black people when he was defending us in speeches or debates on television. He was exceptional, for lack of a better word.

Michael Eric Dyson showed me that I could be black and still be accepted by the mainstream, but I didn't have to be one of the mainstream. Although he is very candid in the way he talks about race, culture, and class, he does it in a high-class fashion that allows him to connect with people from a multitude of cultural experiences. While under the indirect tutelage of his guidance, I began to channel my inner Dyson when I began to work at my local courthouse.

While working at the courthouse, I began to be surrounded by a new class of people on an everyday basis, including judges, lawyers, law enforcement workers, and other individuals who were involved in legal and criminality fields. Coming into this territory in March of 2014 was challenging because I began to be bombarded with right-wing Republicans, neoliberalists, and extreme liberals. It also didn't help that my start date occurred a few months prior to the death of Michael Brown and the emerging popularity of the Black Lives Matter movement.

I was not only the sole black male in the office, but I was also one of the youngest. I've considered myself to be very liberal and progressive, so this environment made me check some of my own views. Being one of two people in the office with a college degree put me in a position that motivated people to ask me a fecundity of questions regarding current events, and most of them touched on intraracial crime, police brutality, racism, and politics.

I remained fairly quiet until September, about a month after the protests in Ferguson that sparked worldwide organized resistance against police brutality across the globe. One day I was speaking to a coworker regarding another employee who happened to be an extreme liberal. She frequently felt it was necessary to inform me of her love of President Obama, the name Tyrone, her husband who attended school in North Omaha (a predominantly black area in Omaha), and everything else that was black. I expressed how these innocuous comments were race based, but in a benevolent manner. I remained like President Obama in the first half of presidency by avoiding the subject of race, but this sparked my conservative coworker to ask me about why the killing of Michael Brown was justified.

Apparently the allegations of him stealing cigars warranted enough reason for him to be a thug and ultimately to be executed in the middle of the street with little to no regard. He was just another thug who needed to be off the street anyway because he did not comply with the de facto rules of the establishment. I began to discuss the fancy academic terms from implicit bias to structural institutionalized racism, but she refused to listen. She began to talk about how she didn't care whether people were white, black, yellow, red, or purple because she doesn't see color. I always get kind of weary and dismissive of people once they begin to talk about the mythical purple people that we don't see. I knew I wouldn't convince her or anyone of that matter that day, or even the next day, but from that day forward I made a conscious effort to use my overbearing presence of perceived black exceptionalism to defend my truth and to be a beacon of truth in the workplace.

While Malcolm and other black nationalists preached about the importance of separatism and blacks having their own, they failed to accurately address the importance of having blacks integrate the private and government sectors. While blacks are a huge minority in these spaces, it is important for us to engage with the dominant society by challenging them so that they can be hospitable to minorities and the interests of minorities in the future. Blacks who are deemed exceptional are needed to elevate the status of other blacks. They are also essential in raising the social and racial conscience of the majority.

Working in white-dominated workplaces is more than just a sanctuary that provides a steady paycheck. It also allows me to challenge myself in the manner in which I engage with others and to change the scope of how blackness is viewed. Once we get the majority culture, and even post-racial minorities, to step out of their epistemological closets of parochialism to see that one's cultural identity should not be confined into mainstream standards, then this opens room for progress. Black exceptionalism should not make others think that person is so articulate, well dressed, proper, and intelligent and that he or she isn't like the rest of those Negroes. Instead, it should serve in a purpose that challenges people to understand why they have these preconceived notions of others.

When blacks accept this myopic view of exceptionalism that the dominant society applies to those who fall outside of their stereotypical narrative it becomes dangerous. It perpetuates this convoluted paradigm of black culture being deviant and unworthy of being celebrated within the American consciousness because blackness is only celebrated when it resembles the tradition of whiteness.

The dichotomy of how blacks and whites view "black exceptionalism" must operate conterminously because we must elevate our communities, but we must also raise the bar of how blackness is viewed within the hegemonic power structure.

While being black and exceptional shouldn't be deemed as excellent, it must be excepted. Creating this notion perpetuates this hierarchy that leaves black people as a permanent underclass. Wanting others to view you as smart isn't sufficient, because there were smart Nazis. Being smart must be championed with the courage in telling the truth.

Being black and exceptional can be taxing and exhausting. Even though it may seem innocuous at times, the achievement of blacks allows us to slowly chip away at the infrastructure of white supremacy.

The higher blacks rise, the less color they see. Once you are allowed into these spaces, you have two options: you can be compliant to black individualism, or you can reach back to those communities who marvel at you and to those who may never climb the heights you've flown above.

To whom much is given, much is expected.

CHAPTER 14

THE BLACK EDUCATED CLASS

The term *middle* *class* is looked at as ambiguous because it has no clear definition. One can say it was a term that was popularized in the United States to make people feel more involved within the political context. For the sake of this essay, I would like to classify it as a term associated with those who have benefited from delayed gratification, higher education, home ownership, secure employment, and professional titles. More importantly, I would like to focus on the black middle/educated class. In some contexts it isn't necessary to use the terms synonymously, but in regards to black people, they almost at all times go hand in hand.

Many scholars and historians credit the rapid surge of what we now know as the black middle/educated class to the elimination of *de jure* and the softening of de facto segregation in the late 1960s. This is in no way an attempt to discredit the thriving black communities in Tulsa, Oklahoma; Richmond, Virginia; and in Durham, North Carolina. The important difference in comparison with those communities is that the businesses located within those areas were black owned. This new era of black professionals who gained prominence following the civil rights movement don't own the means of production, but their status puts them above lower tier workers within a company or institution.

The issue regarding this expanded class of black folks is not based on them having careers integrated within the hegemonic power structure, but on the sense of cowardice that seems to come with it—cowards in the sense that members who join these ranks begin to lose their social conscience because they are afraid of losing their status. They become more concerned with their account balance rather than holding themselves accountable for something greater. When this type of philosophy occurs, individuals become prisoners inside their internal jail cells with the inability to birth possibilities for those who are marginalized.

When we look at greed through the guise of whiteness, it can be seen as socioeconomic dominance, but under the umbrella of blackness, it can be perceived within an alternate construct. For instance, since ownership among blacks is so low and almost nonexistent, our greed has us racing for scraps. So in turn this class of black people inherit this innate fear of not making enough or having it taken away. In reality most of the professionals are one layoff away from being the working-class black people that many seem to despise on the surface level.

To elucidate that assertion a good way is to look at the current state of affairs by focusing on birds. Think in terms of migrating geese that are known for flying in their typical V pattern when they are migrating to their breeding (summer) and nonbreeding (winter) homes. One could argue that I'm using a false equivalence to usher in a point, but that collectiveness is missing among us. Instead, this newly fifty-year-old class of black individuals operates like peacocks. Peacocks, on the other hand, aren't much different, and this is not to say that black people should operate in the same manner, but peacocks strut because they can't fly. They have the ability to fly, but due to their large wings, they are unable to sustain the wherewithal to stay in flight for very long. These peacocks, like some in this new black educated class, are only good for claiming their status, money, and material things. Even within black leadership we see members whose commitment started out spreading their wings for justice, but just like the peacock, after a short flight they came back to the ground. These peacocks should be indicted within the court of public blackness for their ethical and moral violence against our people.

When you look in communities that have a significant percentage of black people, you will likely see several organizations that operate as advocates for black people. Most, if not all, of these organizations are nonprofit, but they still strive for profits at the end of the day. In retrospect, when you look at the March on Washington, which many remember as the day that infamous "I Have a Dream" speech was delivered, you saw the Big Six present, coming together for something that was bigger than themselves as individuals. Even though a lot of internal discrimination occurred with erasure of women, the individual still did not dominate the message that was being delivered.

At times when I look at different organizations that I've worked with and volunteered for, one prominent factor existed among them, and that was the fact that they basically all strived for the same thing. Most organizations' core values are aimed at education, employment opportunities, and keeping kids off the street. Even though they are black groups striving for the same cause, they ultimately fall short of corroding these deadly cancers that affect us as a group. I won't argue that our community is lacking proper planning, instead, I would argue that it's the abundance of leadership. I don't see how pragmatic it is to have several organizations that vie to do the exact same thing. Instead of partnering up to intensify their effectiveness, they begin to see competition among the leaders of these groups—competition in the sense of getting endorsements that may also include financial ones from philanthropy groups and government budgets. Once you prostitute yourself to get outside funding, you slowly give away your control, because your organization becomes dependent on where the money is flowing from. This, however, can create a meritocracy among minority groups where peacocks begin to breed more peacocks.

We started off trying to build our own, but this type of financial inclusion allows the hegemonic society to systematically infiltrate through philanthocracy, which is the rule of tyranny of people who give their money and fame to causes. Instead of trying to reach every child possible, you notice that some groups that deal mainly with youth only seem to recruit those who fit a certain kind of mold. You mainly see the gifted children being reached out to, instead of the most troubled youth who may be at the lower end of the curve. Even though every child is precious, once you divorce from your original foundation and create a youthful meritocracy, you begin to sell yourself out. We begin to create a dissonance among these bright, gifted children and the rest of them. These children then begin to grow up to repeat these same cycles in their respective fields.

I stated previously that I've worked in some of the organizations I talked about, even though I meticulously failed to name them. I remember working with one of the children and during a one-on-one basketball game, out of frustration over losing the game to me, he began to scream at me that he would end up making more money than me and he would have more degrees than me. The yelling didn't upset me or cause me any consternation because I always tell children that they should never be afraid to express themselves. Releasing negative energy in a way that may come across as recalcitrant is better than keeping it bottled in. Encapsulating your true feelings is always accepted, but this incident sort of rubbed me the wrong way. That incident gave the foundation for this essay. I support our young men and women achieving academic success and financial upward mobility, but I felt he didn't understand that I was only there because I cared. I never sought out to take a vow of poverty, but joining the black bourgeoisie was never a primary goal. Instead, I wanted to give back to what was given for me to achieve.

As we look back on the March on Washington for jobs and freedom, is this really what Martin Luther King Jr. died for? Is this what Rosa Parks sat on that bus for? Did this movement occur so that a segment of blacks could gain status and money so that they shun other black people? Externally, we come off as though we are striving to eradicate the way racial stereotypes are formed. Instead, it seems as though we have internalized those stereotypes. Instead of centering our focus on the underfunding of schools, income inequality, food deserts, health-care disparity, and a fecundity of issues that plague our communities, we begin to play the shame game.

Malcolm X talked about how whites couldn't say they respected him as a person if they didn't respect his brothers or sisters on the block. Even though some of these new black professionals might be first- or even second-generation professionals, they still have close ties to poorer blacks whom they seem to forget about. Instead of becoming advocates for the struggle, they get on their bully pulpit and begin to become an echo chamber for stereotypes that are spewed out from the majority culture. Even though we don't want to be judged as a monolithic race, it comes off as disconcerting because now this new class of educated blacks is looked at as exceptional Negroes, and a blind eye is being turned to the oppression that the majority of blacks are experiencing. A select few are allowed to integrate into this new social world, but my community is still indifferent to you. So in a sense my humanity is still not fully valued and my overall blackness is being compromised.

A lot of the people in the black educated class fall victim to this trap, and they end up overtly or subconsciously selling out to the white power structure. Even though they are still a couple of degrees removed from poverty and despair, they become too afraid and intimidated by the powers that be to take a stand against racial and structural injustices.

On a micro level it would be erroneous to contend that this class of individuals can save Black America, but they can recycle some of their privileges and in-kind services by helping others on a practical level. We shouldn't be against black people, but we should challenge blacks who suffer from Afro-amnesia in a sense that they feel they have transcended race. The black educated class is a sign of progress, but it shouldn't come with black forgetfulness. It's not about what you have. We should be more concerned about what you are doing with it.

The reality is that the black bourgeoisie has turned into a rhetorical stylistic aesthetic of moral hierarchy. No matter if you come from generational wealth, or if you're a few steps out of poverty, the language begins to deem those who are trapped within the confines of poverty as "them other niggas." Now you begin to be pretentious and condescending against the alleged barbaric Negroes in or on the cuffs of poverty who listen to that dreaded "rap music" and who can't tell a dinner fork from one that is used for salads.

While I understand the fundamental importance of the existence of groups like Jack & Jill, let's not forget about Jamal and Leticia. Your worth and value should not be limited to the organization you belong to, but it should be represented by how you use that organization to uplift others who may not ever be considered for membership. These groups are important to the social mobility of black progression and securing the future of Black America, but if your definition of progress is allowing you to possess the ability to be hurtful to other black people, then that is a progress that is dangerous to the collective benefit of black people, and I don't want it. This doesn't insulate you from white supremacy, and it doesn't make you better than those black folk who have been left behind. Black progress is necessary; the expansion of the black-middle class is crucial, but we must not lose sight of our collective struggle by blaming those who don't benefit from upward financial mobility.

We can't claim that those blacks are the sole perpetrators of their failure. Instead, we must treat the struggle of Black America in the form of a triage where we look at the dichotomy of systemic issues while applying the necessary amount of critique to personal responsibility. Black excellence is expected, not exceptional. We can't focus on celebrating those who succeed despite horrid circumstances; instead we must fight for everyone to have ample opportunity at the chance to excel. I'm more concerned about what you are doing with this success.

Taking a vow of poverty is something that shouldn't be asked. Instead, it should be about how your success is peddled into uplifting others. Is your only concern your car, bank account, or what type of suit you have on? Many of these professionals come from communities where they were the first ones to go to college, and when they return, the residents see them as symbols of hope. They are looked at as iconographic figures who have achieved something that many were taught to believe was astronomical.

Whether you want to look at yourself as a role model or not, you still are. Your progress is personal to children from lower middle class and impoverished communities because it gives them the opportunity to see the face of someone who is able to reach out to them. They see entertainers on television, drug pushers, and others using illicit means to get over, but you come back as a different alternative. You're smart, linguistically sound, and charming to them. Your life becomes personal because your face is now ingrained in their mind when they try to imagine a different future. Instead of yellow grass, you're green. No more project windows; instead, you give them hopes of a picket fence. Instead of pushing illegal drugs, you can shape them into being pharmaceutical technicians. Yes, this progress is personal because you're not only filling up your bank accounts, but you're filling up heads with dreams of children who don't have access to another alternative. This myopic individualistic narcissist of being self made is asinine. Somebody prayed, worked, marched, and died for us to be here.

Malcolm once said, "In all our deeds, the proper value and respect for time determines success or failure." The time is now to support one another, no matter how different their statuses are in comparison to ours. You should never be afraid of losing status due to speaking up against those who demonized you, because you may be next.

Martin Luther King spoke these words in his last speech, "I've Been to the Mountaintop," and they still resonate today: "The question is not, if I stop to help this man in need, what will happen to me? If I do not stop to help the sanitation workers, what will happen to them? That's the question."

CHAPTER 15

AMBIVALENT HOMOPHOBIA

The Lesbian, Gay, Bisexual, Transgender, Queer/Questioning (LGBTQ) community has been making momentous and astronomical strides in the fight toward equality in the United States. At this time many would feel that the United States should be proud, but many in this country of ours are getting their heterosexual privileges checked, and some are experiencing heterosexual guilt.

On the surface it's easy to say we support marriage and civil unions for all, but as a person who has lived a life wrapped around religion and intoxicated with a degree of heteronormativity, you begin to feel a sense of sexual ambivalence to an issue that acts as countervailing narrative to the language of sexual relations to which you have been accustomed.

To support these ambivalent or nefarious attitudes toward homosexuality, people hide behind the theological or the biological argument. In a sense they use science and GOD to act as cosigners for their bigotry. Our country has slowly moved toward being a progressive democracy, but on this issue it seems as though many of our citizens have been unmolested by enlightenment and untrammeled of virtue in regards to this issue. This is especially troubling since our nation is more educated than it was upon its founding. This issue turns everyone into biblical literalists and bioethicists. When discussing homosexuality and gay marriage, many argue on the premise of whether same-sex attraction is biological or simply a choice. Many tend to use the choice argument as a fundamental point to defend their dogmas.

When opponents of homosexuality use the law of attraction to profess their views through scripture and the purpose of reproduction, we begin to use relationships as a sole means to bring children into this world, which denotes its use of pleasure not just in a procreation manner. The logic that homosexuality bastardizes the primary function for sex will eliminate various forms of heterosexual activity. In philosophy, a popular formal fallacy is referred to as "affirming the consequent," sometimes called converse error, fallacy of the converse, or confusion of necessity. The general form of the argument is listed below.

If P, then Q.
Q.
Therefore, P.

An argument will always be invalid even if 1 and 2 are correct, but doesn't result in 3 being correct. For instance, if the premise of one's argument is that sex is used for reproduction, then the consequent must always result in a pregnancy. Whenever room is made for illogical fallacies, then we must cogitate about how we think about sexuality and gender. We must step outside these epistemological closets of parochialism.

My personal ambivalence toward homosexuality has never been rooted in theology or biology, but it was solely embedded within the confines of race. This benign neglect of homosexuality is troublesome because it leaves out many brothers and sisters for whom I claim to fight for. While we are in the battle of black upliftment, I and others begin to oppress those who fall outside our heteronormativism. Even though we have historically had homosexuals in our community, it was seen as taboo to talk about it or acknowledge it. We ironically pushed them into the proverbial closet. By not allowing or acknowledging black homosexuals, we begin to become an echo chamber to the same dominant forces we claim we are up against.

Many argue that the plight of racism and homophobia can't be compared due to economic factors that formulated race and the fact that it's highly unlikely that you can hide your race, but that doesn't account for an adequate excuse to why we can't accept people who have an alternative lifestyle to what is deemed the norm by society. Even though we have different sects of blacks within the fight of black liberation, ranging from the church to those whose belief system is embedded within an agnostic spiritual system, many core beliefs have the influence of morality that it derives from religious doctrines.

Even though more and more people are breaking away from traditional religious traditions, people still are imprisoned by the absolute thought of right and wrong. All of life's obstacles are not afforded the chance for deep critical thought, but issues regarding sexuality, something that is worthy of extreme cogitation, seem to be among those topics we just toss to our sub-conscious religious ethics of natural law.

I feel that's one of the reasons society can freely discriminate against gays. I feel as though gay discrimination is prevalent because it's the easiest sin for heterosexuals to avoid. As a society we get so caught up in the theory of "good and bad" that we don't allow for any gray area to deem anything acceptable. I can recall being around ten years old, when my brother told me he had a gay coworker. I vividly remember asking, "Did they fire her?" He explained that's against the law, but as a child it seemed as though I was subconsciously trained to believe that homosexuality was bad and an abomination not only to religion, but also to a stable society in general. Is GOD's word to blame for these thoughts, or is it the religion that man is proselytizing toward us?

I'm notorious for the biblical comment, "I don't know the verse, but I know it's in there." I judge others, even though I know it's against GOD's law, but I do it. I know I sin daily, but knowing I can repent gives me the thought that it will be forgiven. They say GOD is all knowing and makes no mistakes. Why would he make some gay when the act of homosexuality is supposedly against his word, but make the majority of everyone else straight? As in the book of Job, does he allow this to happen to test their faith? Seriously, if you know something is a sin, but you continually act on it, is that sort of like you're rebelling against GOD? Since I'm judging, does GOD equally look down on me as he would look down on gays?

Why don't we as individuals think about why we pick and choose stories out of the Bible to justify our ambivalent views? It's easy because we aren't the subject. The lights aren't on us in the interrogation room, and instead we are just bystanders being blind to the treatment that others are receiving. We will argue up and down in barbershops about Kobe versus LeBron or Michael Jackson versus Prince, but we ignore critical corrections about equal rights that result in us submitting to inegalitarianism through our ambivalence. Sometimes we must ask ourselves poignant questions about the world we live in, even when it steps outside the boundaries of morality by not providing us a right or wrong answer.

Can I change my views on a lifestyle that I'm ignorant to? Why does this heterosexual privilege give me the constabulary theological justification to convey to others how GOD wants them to act? We have conservatives and religious officials trying to exorcise people over what they feel is a decision. They try to use religion as a divine cure and treatment. So if GOD makes no mistakes, then why are we allowing man-made rewiring of GOD's work? Why can't homosexuals be allowed the same human privileges that I enjoy? The government says they try to separate church from state, but how can one separate his religion from this sin in particular? How can we bridge the gap? Will GOD judge me for being cool with those of different sexual orientations if it's supposedly against his word? However, the Bible tells you to love all your neighbors. These contradicting messages in a man-written book continue to perpetuate these mixed feelings.

The struggle of trying to advocate for a lifestyle I'm not involved in may seem easy for those who are waving the different flags, in the streets marching, and consistently fighting for equality, but for a man who has nothing to gain, it's difficult to find the piece of the puzzle where you fit in. Rights should be for all people, no matter who they are or the practices that they exercise, but you'd be a fool not to notice that segregation among people of separate orientations is still apparent to a certain extent. Is it possible to completely endorse a lifestyle, but still be uncomfortable at times surrounded by it, or even talking about it? The Supreme Court decision in favor of marriage equality for all produced a proliferation of Facebook profile pictures draped in rainbow colors to show solidarity.

In response, several black liberation flags began to drape profile pictures. In a sense, it felt as though some were trying to combat homosexuality, but it also felt as though this was a joyous sign of freedom. Blacks shouldn't lose sight of the ongoing battle against state violence.

I've never considered myself an ally or an agitator. I've always felt as though it wasn't my place to give an opinion. I would encompass an uneasy feeling when I would see posts disparaging or poking fun at gay people, but I would never respond. At times I felt like it was none of my business, but other times I felt as though I was excusing the treatment of oppression against people of the world. While gay and lesbians are trying to walk out of those closets of their own condemnation so that they can express themselves freely, I'm still stuck in my own proverbial closet of heterosexual guilt.

Heterosexual privilege is very common, even though you may not realize it. I can talk about sexual relations, and I won't be judged for it. The most that people will say is that the place where speaking on it isn't appropriate. I'm not segregated due to my preference. I won't get stared at while on dates because me taking a woman out is "normal." I'm never looked at as the straight guy. I'm judged by my circumstances, my character, and the ethics I represent. I never have to explain the image in which GOD made me. All that seems well and good until you start feeling like you're a part of the problem.

When you're constantly telling yourself that gay equality is an issue you shouldn't be involved in because it's not your struggle, when does that make you just as guilty as those people protesting and screaming faggot? I don't want to be that straight black guy marching, surrounded by a bunch of rainbow-colored flags. I don't want to make others uncomfortable. Why should I care about helping gay and lesbians live in a world that accepts them? It's not my issue! You get those voices telling you that if you stand up for gays, what will others think of you? Nobody wants to be the one suspected as the "closet faggot."

How can I be the black man who fights for freedom of equality for those who share my pigmentation, but refuses to even stand up and say equality should be for all, no matter the color or sexual preference? How can I accept gays being looked at in the United States as the lesser when there was a time when the open treatment toward gays was openly practiced by those who resemble me? Those who sit when they have the option to stand up are no better than the ones who scream words such as "faggot," "homo," and "dyke."

Over the past few years, I understand that we all come from the same creator and we all deserve the same chance at the same opportunities. Whenever we crack open room for discrimination in any place, then we open the door for discrimination everywhere. No laws can change society's views. The only thing that can change the way of the world is us. Once you take away the fear and hate, you'd be surprised to find that love is underneath. That holy water that GOD made us has become poisoned. If we are judged, ridiculed, or accused of being a closet fag, then it should give us no worries because equality for all, no matter race, gender, or sexual orientation are issues that need to be supported by all. Even though this is one of a countless number of sins broken daily in the Bible, sometimes you just put your personal views aside and support the betterment of society. Isn't this the reason Jesus died anyway, for the sins of his people?

I don't root my feelings about homosexuality in religion or biology, but I think that many, including myself, have ambivalent beliefs in homosexuality that are rooted within our own narcissism. We only see oppression through our own myopic prisms, and jealousy begins to occur once we feel we are left out of the liberation movement.

Too often people try to categorize moments like this as a way to distract us from other incidents such as Charleston, Baltimore, Ferguson, Staten Island, and the other countless cities that have a nationwide spotlight on them regarding racial and state violence. By aligning ourselves with this thought process, in a sense we limit ourselves to be singular thinkers, instead of being a people that can be multifaceted in our thinking. We must be like an iconoclast in how we demolish this way of thinking because of the intersectionality that exists among some black people who allow their multiple struggles to act conterminously.

The black story or struggle is not one that is monotonous within one singular issue, while the issue of racial discrimination is poignant. But if we allow discrimination on other fronts among our brother and sisters, then we allow them to be alienated and lost from the movement. We must find a way for them to be embraced because our strength is rooted within us operating as a collective.

Some of us live different lifestyles, pray to alternate GODs, and look at sexuality different, but we all share the same goal of living in a world that is free from oppression and rooted in equality.

CHAPTER 16

A Letter to My Sister

Dear Sister,

Many men profess their love to you by referring to you as a queen. Even though on the surface it may seem genuine and many may have good intentions when they place this iconographic label on you, I would like you to be aware that I feel you are always enough, even when you may not live up to unrealistic expectations that others may place on you.

The label of queen is almost always used as a machination to restrict women and young girls to a status of respectability to enslave them to a notion of how a woman is supposed to behave under the male guise. Not only does it limit them equally to their male counterparts, but it also limits their right to define their femininity by placing it within a tightly quarantined paradigm.

I am aware of the history of black women tearing through the fabrics of patriarchy to lead in the ways that Ella Baker, Sojourner Truth, Harriet Tubman, Angela Davis, Margaret (Peggy) Jones, and many others have done. Instead of restricting your limits of what you can do, I, in addition to other black men, have a greater responsibility to you.

In no way am I trying to say one voice is more legitimate than another, but one of the most powerful things is when a black man uses his voice to uplift his black sister. When society refuses to hear your voices, we must use our privilege to articulate and to convey your message to the masses. While black women have no issue making their sentiments known even in the most dire of circumstances, we still have a responsibility to alleviate the load of suffering and oppression that you and others face.

I love you, but my love for you should always be presented with respect of not just you as a human, but also with respect for the struggle that women like yourself endure daily. Too many men think they are not contributing to oppression of women because we open doors and we don't call them derogatory names, rape them, or hit them. While those aforementioned actions are reprehensible, we must be conscious of the fact that simply saying we are against sexism, misogyny, and patriarchy on a surface level isn't enough. I may not call you a bitch or a ho, but if I try to put you in your place or subordinate you to a man-made restriction, then I'm treating you like a dog and raping you of the equal opportunity that my masculinity affords me.

I don't want to take up too much of your time, but just know that you are loved and that I'm here to protect you if need be. I hope you never hesitate to hit me up. If it's an issue that you don't feel comfortable telling me, I'll most likely have female resources I can pass you to. I hope you never feel that you are in this world all by yourself.

Love always,

Brandon C. Lovelace

CHAPTER 17

The Pain in Being a Strong Black Woman

As an adult I cannot think of a time when I witnessed my mother crying. I know we all express internal pain in times of sorrow, but it seems as though she would never allow anyone to see in her a vulnerable place. I've never seen my mother exhibit frustration unless it was with her disappointment in me. Back then I placed the onus of her anger on me. Now I'm beginning to realize that it may be a direct frustration with her, in the belief that she may have failed. Even though my father was active in my life, he wasn't in the household, so my living space was matriarchal. His presence was felt, but she was still the point guard guiding me as a youth.

Since the sixties leading into the seventies, black households have increasingly been headed by a woman, and even before the sixties, black mothers bore the responsibility of taking care of homes during slavery, with little help. Many factors are at play when you look at the increased number of single-parent households nationally, not just in the segment of black households, but throughout all races in the United States. Historically, black women have taken on the roles of superheroes. As heads of these modern households, they are wearing hats that traditionally shouldn't fit: holding down a full-time job (sometimes multiple ones) and bearing the sole responsibility of raising boys into men and girls into women. Not only are these single mothers supposed to be nurturers, but they are also our protectors.

Just as in previous generations, black women today have grown up with the assumption that they have to play a superhero role in a society where they have to show their strength all the time and not show any signs of vulnerabilities. Superheroes should only exist in comic books and in movies, but by taking on this heroic role, black women are cheating themselves out of a life of normalcy and complete happiness.

By taking on the superhero "I can do it on my own" persona, you sacrifice taking care of your own needs. We as a black community have imprisoned many of our sisters into these roles instead of letting them be free to define who they truly can be, instead of the infamous single mother of two who has to work two to three jobs just to keep the lights on. Before we can even look at ways of fixing these roles that we have trapped a lot of these women in, we have to see those factors that have led to the hardened black feminine superhero figure.

It would be dishonest not to acknowledge other determining factors such as mass incarceration, unemployment, and economic disparities as issues that place women into these roles; we must be honest in how we don't allow safe spaces for black women to be vulnerable in expressing grief. They are expected to not only be the backbone to their families, but they must also bear the burden of being the heartbeat as well. Black women are required to nurture everyone and provide shoulders for relief, but whom are they allowed to turn to in their moment of despair?

I can recall times visiting loved ones who were locked up and being astounded by the things I witnessed in the visiting room. I can always recall seeing men being visited by their significant others every time I visited an inmate. No matter how long their bid was, someone they loved romantically always made a conscious effort to be there, even if all they could provide was just a loving touch or the glimpse of hope that someone still cared. The times I spent visiting female inmates revealed something quite different. These black women rarely, if at all, had their male counterparts there. Even though I didn't do field interviews for these women, it would be hard to believe that these women didn't feel abandoned. When we look at the rate of mass incarceration, black women are the fastest rising group, but they still aren't shown the same compassion that black males receive. The shoulders that they provide are reciprocated with cold ones.

We must ask ourselves why she feels the need to be strong and to put on this mask of a strong heroic woman. Under that mask of strength, fearlessness, and confidence could be a woman who grew up fatherless, one who was raped or abused, or who had to witness a mother being abused physically or emotionally by a significant other. A lot of these issues that many women try to hide are usually the determining factors of their character. Many of our sisters are covered in smiles that conceal broken hearts, fear of failure, and despair.

Too often the word *strong* is used to label black women as superhuman because we have this false epistemological belief that they can endure more pain than the average human being. It can be argued that black women endure more abuse than any other group on earth, which makes it easier for physical, emotional, and physiological abuse to be inflicted upon them. This notion to be strong for the sake of their blackness, families, and communities turns them into warriors who at the end of the day cannot even be honest with themselves about the trauma they are experiencing. This type of pain begins to become normalized, which in turn takes away from the opportunity for it to be medicalized. While in a community these feats of heroism are celebrated among black women, we turn a blind eye to the issues that ultimately put them in these compromising binds. Instead of creating spaces where black women are allowed to roam freely, we instead put them into these unrealistic expectations of struggle that we assert onto our women as a rite of passage.

Black women are required to make a dollar out of fifteen cents, and even when income inequality is discussed among men and women, the disparities that black women face are generally always erased from the conversation. While we consistently talk about how white women make seventy-seven cents for every dollar that a white man makes, we forget to acknowledge that black women only make sixty-four cents. A black woman's voice should be heard, instead of being silenced. They are deemed strong enough to make a way and tough enough to constantly shrug off the discrimination they face. The strength of a black woman should be used a mechanism for progression, not as a crutch to excuse discrimination.

We understand that being black and being female in a world that functions under the system of white male patriarchy is challenging, because they are trapped within the margins of multiple oppressions simultaneously. We expect black women to encamp themselves in a singular group, which perpetuates this notion of black women taking care of everyone but themselves. When we ask black women to tackle gender issues, their race is generally marginalized. However, when they are asked to fight for a race issue, then they are asked to dismiss their femininity because it compromises the current grapple that is ensuing.

The issue is that we can't expect someone to give herself to others without any reciprocity for herself. For these women who are forced to be the backbone and the heartbeat to communities, we pass on these beliefs to younger generations that women must look out for the needs of the community first and their personal care second.

We must ask ourselves why we view the black women in our lives as strong—whether they are our mothers, grandmothers, aunts, teachers, wives, girlfriends, or even our fictive kin. Where does this admiration come from? Too often we focus on their triumphs, and we don't exhibit any compassion concerning their struggles. Black women are looked at as individuals who wear bulletproof vests. While others run at the sight of gunfire, black women are expected to face these bullets that life shoots at them with full force. So instead of focusing on their personal wounds, they must put on a Band-Aid and focus on being teachers, nurses, counselors, psychologists, mothers, and cooks to the community.

In addition to everything else that comes with the territory, we allocate less time for black women to grieve and suffer; their agony is deemed less important because of the erroneous expectations that we place upon them. We only care about sprinters crossing the finish line, but we never speak about the painful training and work regiments that are prerequisites for these accomplishments.

Why we applaud black women for all that they have to endure and for their abilities, I feel it's disingenuous not to ask what we can do about the scars they receive. When do we give these women a shoulder to cry on, an ear that will listen, and a heart that will beat for them? When will we remove the load off their back instead of requesting that they build stronger backs? By allowing these mythological notions that black women must be strong, we're allowing them to underappreciated, overworked, and exploited just because these burdens have been placed on them historically.

Black women need to be afforded the opportunity to cry and grieve openly without being shamed to the degree that they feel that they've not only let down their community, gender, race, and their families, but ultimately themselves too.

Even though "strong" black women have produced college graduates and upstanding citizens, and have progressed our communities—while many of our black men were strung out on drugs, walked away, or populated the prison systems—it seems that the "the strong black woman" has done more hurt to herself and left her own personal happiness unfilled. Even when the world seems to be against her, she still manages to find compassion to propel forward not only her house and community, but also the world.

CHAPTER 18

Words Matter

In 1993 Queen Latifah released an album called *Black Reign*. This disk birthed the song "U.N.I.T.Y.," which impregnated society with more contemporary discourse regarding the word *bitch*. Not only did it win a Grammy in 1995, but it also challenged the moral consciousness of the urban United States by discussing the issues of street harassment, domestic violence, and slurs against women in hip-hop culture.

In every generation we seem to notice a fecundity of people who are liberated by the tongue with their use of the word *bitch*, especially those who happen to be male. One can argue that even when women attempt to reclaim the word, they are still in a sense reinforcing the sexism and patriarchy from which the word derives. However, I feel that when we try to reprimand women for their usage, we begin to commit erasure against the oppressive nature in which men use the word.

Folklore taught us that "sticks and stones may break our bones, but words will never hurt me." This happens to promote a dangerous narrative. We must begin to teach that words aren't coterminous with physical pain. Words matter! Too often we concentrate on a litany of arguments that focus on the images that are presented, while ignoring the words that are associated with them. Images are meaningless when we extract the words that become ingrained in our heads when we view them. Images become osmosis in how we encapsulate in the meaning of words and the subjects they are related to. How we identify words are salient to our generally consensus of identity. The term *bitch* may seem innocuous on the surface, but it erases the existential permanence of a woman's being.

We live in not only a nation, but also a world that is male-dominated and that provides spaces of authority that are generally reserved for men. One can always argue that women are rapidly creating individual agency and occupying spaces that were historically reserved for males. Even though patriarchy isn't explicit at times and can come off as innocuous, it's very legerdemain in its functions. When things are centered around the male guise, then everything that is masculine is considered normal, good, and the unequivocal standard. Even if you're not explicitly referring to a woman as a bitch, if you subordinate a woman to a man-made restriction, you may not be calling her that epithet, but you are treating her like one. So, even though all men may not be in higher positions than all women, patriarchy reinforces this notion that they are their superior. When we look at how the word *bitch* is articulated from a sociological context on the premise of patriarchy and within the constraints of the inequalities that women face, we begin to understand how words operate on a functional equivalence to that of physical harm that women also endure.

Words aren't just messages that can be jotted down on a piece of paper or heard through a radio; words can make or break the self-esteem of a person. So when we look at the words *queen, women, girls,* and *female,* they seem to describe essentially the same thing. In a sense they do that, but when we look at each word individually and begin to create a more concrete analysis, we begin to notice their subtle difference and the nuances among them. *Queen* can describe a woman of royalty or of a high social apparatus. *Woman* is generally used to describe a lady that is of an adult age, while *girl* is used to identify ladies who are young. When we look at the word *female,* it doesn't define a human in absolute terms, but instead it can describe any organism that happens to be female. So when we look at the word *bitch*, people always attempt to justify its meaning. Some will argue that all women aren't bitches, and if a woman knows she isn't one, then she has no reason to be offended. From an etymological perspective, the word *bitch* is used to describe female foxes, otters, and most knowingly, dogs. No matter how we view man's proverbial best friend, at the end of the day, man and dog know they don't eat at the same table.

Once we commit to allowing women to be acknowledged by something other than *human*, then we begin to erase their human nature and deplete their existence. We are using words as a way to systematically erase them. Sociology teaches that the more names we have for things, the more value they have. But by having several words that are derogatory toward women, we are also showing how much we feel they are beneath us.

In this system of patriarchy that encompasses us, *bitch* can be seen as the lowest of lows. Even when it's not directly used to refer to a woman, it is also used to refer to moments of destitution and sexual slavery. In rap we often hear how bitch is used as a metaphor or a colloquialism for troubles of life, whether it's Nas articulating about how life's a bitch, or Kanye speaking on how life is a bitch and he wants to make it cum. Either bitches make our life difficult, or they are used for some sort of sexual gratification. Even Pac metaphorically spoke in "Me & My Bitch," a song in which *bitch* was used as colloquialism for a gun, a gun he owned.

In the previous examples that are talked about, those uses of the word *bitch* were for ownership, struggle, and dominance.

When we look at this term, we must be perspicacious in how it works as a machination for the way women are viewed and valued. Previously I talked about how people, men especially, attempt to argue that women shouldn't get offended if they know they are not bitches, but the language predisposes you to believe a certain type of value is attached to the person in question. For example, what makes a woman a bitch or a nonbitch? What factors are at play that allow you to determine how one is defined? In most instances it seems these labels are attached to women once they step outside the boundaries or realms of what men expect of them. Women can be referred to as such when they don't cooperate with men, or when they are seen as manipulative and deviant in how they attract certain men. When *bitch* is used synonymously with the word *women*, this causes females to be looked at as something that must be conquered.

This essay is just an abstract of bigger issues that revolve around a word that was uncomfortable for me to write because of the social implications it places on women in the context of patriarchy and heteronormativity. I took a personal vow that I would never refer to any person, especially any woman, by this term because of my hatred for it.

Even though in writing I reference it, I refuse to speak it. I probably was in the third grade when I first referred to a classmate as one in conversation with a male counterpart. I had no issue with her, but as a child the proverbial cool thing to do was to treat girls like the grass beneath your shoe. Looking back in retrospect, I am still ashamed of that choice of language because it was random. Even to this day, I have no justification for it. Even though no reasons exist for me to use it, period, on that day after school it flowed off my lips very casually. In a sense, at a young age I became desensitized to the word.

Even though words change and carry different connotations, that word is still deeply rooted in hurt, trauma, and desecration. Sexism in the world has become the norm, even though women are making great strides within the male consciousness. We as men are still allowing those tears that women have cried to turn into sexist oceans that we swim in freely.

How can we fight for freedom for all when we ignore the lack of liberation for some? Words matter. *Bitch* still promotes the notion that women are different from men and will always remain his proverbial best friend—good enough to love, pet, and care for, but never good enough to eat from the same table. Bitches are only allowed his scraps.

CHAPTER 19

FORMULATING HER IDENTITY

In the terms of gender identity, most experts, if you ask them, will likely come to a majority consensus that one's sense of what it is to be a man or woman is determined by society—aside from sex organs, of course. I would like to ask whether black women determine who they are, or do men make that decision? More importantly, what is the black man's role in it, so we can unravel this conundrum about the intersections of race and gender.

When a white man looks in the mirror, he sees himself as a human. A white woman likely will see herself as a woman. A black man will identify with his blackness, but where do black women fall into the archetype of this mirror? What does a black woman identify with? Is it their race or their gender, and why are their sexualities being primed when we think of them? One of the main issues in answering these questions is that people are too comfortable with the norm. We as a community, male and female, need to understand what is reflecting back to us, and plan to break the mirror that doesn't give black women a right to choose what roles they identify with.

At early ages black girls are taught that their bodies are their temples and that they must be protected. When we begin to prime a girl's body, we're reinforcing these stereotypes that a woman's body is her most important asset. A black woman at one time was only useful for manual house labor and reproduction. Now modern-day images of Sarah Baartmen have transitioned from pornography to the mainstream with the intent of profit for corporations, while black men are used as pawns to exploit and degrade black and brown women. Like an old saying, women are made to think that their only future is behind them—not in the sense of the past, but in the sense of their gluteus maximus.

Women essentially have a choice in the matter of whether their bodies will be used as a commodity or something that has no direct correlation on how they will be financially compensated, but a patriarchy-governed society in most cases can overpower the desires she wants for herself.

We can look at higher paying careers in which a woman's intellect is more primed, even then she is judged on a higher ceiling and has to push through a heavier door. Physical beauty is good, physical beauty is great. I would never tell a girl to be ashamed of that, nor will I tell her that you should feel guilty of the image GOD created you in. But when physical beauty is a means to an end of success, we then begin to idolatrize the financial gain and the pleasure that a woman's body can provide, which eventually leads us to avoid her intellect. We also see this with of a lot of the women we force girls to look up to. For example, when we look at someone that is as beautiful as Gabrielle Union, we are aware that she has been in multiple films and her own series, but we always seem to focus on her beauty. We almost always disregard the fact that she has a sociology degree from the University of Nebraska–Lincoln.

When these images are pushed on not only girls, but also boys as well, then this begins to stunt our growth, because even though we may not have a direct connection with these people, we're still looking at them as role models—not for the smarts they may have, but only their beauty.

A lot of these girls grow up without fathers or other male figures in their lives that can show them a type of love that isn't romanticized. Girls growing up need to experience love from a man that is sensual, instead of love that has an expectation when it is given to our young women. Many of us instill in our young ladies that they need to love themselves, I feel as though that isn't enough. For people to develop healthy social lives, they need to know what love is and what it feels like. When a girl isn't receiving that type of attention from a father figure, she may feel as though she isn't good enough or she's worthless. This may begin a process where she feels as though any attention from any guy is sufficient, even though at times that attention may be given with ill intentions. We see these scenarios too often in music and film where a black woman's role is to be oversexualized.

Many people might try to counter the notion that we don't complain when white women are in these realms. To answer those critics, I feel it's important to note that you can go to different arenas and outside media to see white women in different roles that don't highlight their sexuality, but channel their smarts and brains. I have no issues with women of color being sexual objects, but when we see a trend of that being the only light we see them in, then we must combat this problem. We as men and women have become too comfortable and complacent in seeing women as sexual beings instead of seeing them as free, brave, and fighting these oppressive practices. Of course we shouldn't deny the beauty on the outside, but what about her soul, heart, and cerebral capacity? A lot of women are reduced to complying with stereotypes to make a substantial living, but instead, as a society we need to open up additional avenues of opportunity for women to explore other paths that highlight their analytical ability, instead of reducing them to video models, strippers, some man's eye candy, or a trophy wife.

In this patriarchal society a woman is taught that her body is a temple, but not something precious—instead, it's a means to an end. However, when we send our boys off into the world, we sometimes jokingly tell them to "Go out and get up on these hoes," but we tell women that they have to earn their way. How can we expect boys to do one thing, while we tell women to be saints who are pure? We have men who walk around with this sense of entitlement and women being shamed if they feed into what we sell our boys. We are subconsciously elevating our boys into the roles of pimps, one of the most misogynistic people to ever walk the earth.

By doing that we have made a conscious action to reduce women to being hoes and bitches. We can argue that we didn't make the rules and that we are just products of the system, but when you choose to promote these gender stereotypes, you are still guilty of doing something wrong. You're just as guilty as the creator of them.

These practices aren't just in the media and job markets, as I stated earlier, but also in the church that women numerically rule. When a majority of a congregation is female, have we ever wondered why in some churches it's almost taboo for them to rule? Of course we can take their money, but in the end we subjugate submissive roles within the arena of a religious institution. This is not only ecclesiastical apartheid, but it reinforces the classical passive stereotypes and roles we have placed on them.

How can we tell our young girls to go out into the world fearless and to define themselves when we as a society repeatedly devalue them not only in entertainment, but also in the home, classroom, and even when they enter the church? How can we tell black girls that they rock when we are limiting the levels of degrees they can rock in? Studies show that most children conform to gender roles as early as four years old, but who is at fault? Frederick Douglas once said, "It's easier to train young boys than to fix broken men." Let's make a philosophical shift. If we aren't fixing the males in our community, how can we expect more of our young women?

Who really wants to see our young ladies of color excel? Who's really pushing them to achieve all that is possible without expecting anything in return? When we ask, "Why do you love black women," does your answer place them in a sexual paradigm, or does it articulate her intellect, acuity, and/or strength? We must figure out who is truly the problem. Is it the girl dancing on the pole or the men who first proclaimed that a woman's most precious part is her temple?

CHAPTER 20

LOVING BLACK WOMEN IN PUBLIC

"Tell them about the dream, Martin." These words were yelled by Mahalia Jackson from her seat in 1963 at the March on Washington. "Black Lives Matter" is a popular slogan created by Alicia Garza, Patrisse Cullors, and Opal Tometi.

I love to see women take individual or collective agency for themselves, but it becomes a revolutionary love once you see black men praise and defend them openly in an unapologetic manner. Cornel West often states that justice is what love looks like in public. I would take it a step further and profess that respect and love are truly expressed when they are unequivocally expressed to those who try to diminish or dwarf it. Too often black women are treated as singular human beings, instead of being within a multifaceted context. They are expected to focus solely on their blackness, sacrificing their womanhood to devote their attention to racial issues that in most instances exclude them from being acknowledged in the forefront.

When we focus on the current movement across the nation against brutality at the hands of police and vigilantes, the names of Trayvon Martin, Eric Garner, Tamir Rice, Freddie Gray, Walter Scott, Akai Gurley, Dontre Hamilton, John Crawford III, Ezell Ford, Phillip White, and Eric Harris come to mind. One of the underlying problematic things that's troubling about those victims is not only that they were killed, but that we also seem to erase black women from the narrative. As a community when we are fighting oppression, we at times oppress others within our own community, simultaneously.

Sometimes as men it's a hard truth to grasp and grapple with. Black men know the struggles that we have to endure daily at the hands of stereotypes, systemic racism and white supremacy, but we often have a blind eye to the oppression in our own home.

While we see countless images of black women showing up on the frontlines bearing witness to our struggles for our men and boys, we don't demonstrate that same assertiveness when it's their lives that are on the line, and we don't show up in the same capacity. The names of Rekia Boyd, Aiyana Jones, Yvette Smith, Pearlie Golden, Tarika Wilson, Shantel Davis, Tyisha Miller, Kathryn Johnston, and Alexia Christian seem to go unnoticed. We allow these names to get erased from our memory and dismissed from the narrative of Black Lives Matter. As black men we don't just bear the responsibility of loving black women in private, but we must remonstrate our cognitive wiring to animadvert their oppression so that they know and feel that they are loved in public.

In Malcolm X's famous speech, "Who Taught You to Hate Yourself," he extemporaneously stated, "The most disrespected woman in America is the black woman. The most un-protected person in America is the black woman. The most neglected person in America is the black woman." When we create a culture of ignoring the violence against women that occurs simultaneously with the violence that is levied upon us, we give others the go-ahead to commit these atrocities because the abusers know they will go unchecked, whether the perpetrator is white or nonwhite. Black men telling black women to sit down in the same manner that Mahalia Jackson was treated during the March of Washington is not only disconcerting, but it also creates a convoluted movement that causes black women to experience cognitive dissonance because they are told their blackness matters, but just not in the scope of priority when it comes to the thinking process of black men.

Black oppression has no gender. Since we live in a patriarchal society, we give these movements male attributes to provide a sense of self-identification. When we uphold the masculine constructs and refuse to allow women prominent roles and visibility within the canon, we don't allow black women to be viewed in a conterminous way with black men.

When we allow this shifting in our paradigms, we begin to excavate the very notions that we uphold of what a black woman's role is. So when we look at our women, we must not just limit them to being trophy pieces. Instead, we must vociferously assert their intelligence, strength, and leadership into the forefront of these movements that we allow to ignore them. This is why loving and respecting black women in public is so important, because once we silence our voices to the masses, we allow women to become complicit to patriarchy.

We must be conscious of the esthetic apartheid that black women and girls have to experience throughout their lives. When you don't see yourself in a positive light on television, on the radio, within print ads, on runways, and in equal numbers within high places of power, you begin to see yourself as less moral, intelligent, and beautiful. The dearth of representation in these key areas can have even the strongest woman questioning her own worth. We teach black women to be strong in the face of adversity and oppression, but in most instances we don't put in that effort to show that they matter for whom they are. We can't critique women who follow a path to find existential acceptance in a form that is appeasing to the standard thinking of man, which in turn may drown out her own values. Who's really willing to stand up and say, "Black women, you matter!" It's not enough to love black women privately, but it is our moral virtue to stand up in the face of the opposition that shuns them.

When we think about the Southern Christian Leadership Conference (SCLC) and Student Nonviolent Coordinating Committee (SNCC) and we don't talk about the influence and leadership from Ella Baker, we aren't being honest. We can't talk about the anti-lynching movement without acknowledging the leadership of Ida B. Wells-Barnett. Nannie Helen Burroughs, Mary Church Terrell, Jo Ann Robinson, and many others gave testimony and put in the work to provide the freedoms we enjoy, but they somehow go unnoticed when we speak of great black American figures. It is a mendacious act to ignore the contributions of women who have fought for us while we enjoy the fecundity of fruits that have been bestowed for us.

While it's important to shine light on Rosa Parks, it's very dishonest to coin her as the mother of the freedom movement, because it may come off as benevolent. In reality, it adjudicates and excavates those who fought for our freedom previously. While her contributions are worthy of cogitation and praise, focusing just on Parks promotes this notion of black female exceptionalism, instead of showing how ubiquitous black female achievement is. Her act of civil disobedience was exceptional. It does not, however, erase the same act that was done previously by Claudette Colvin, as if other women didn't do extraordinary things for black movements. This, however, is the result of black men refusing to step down or to the side of their bully pulpits to make room for their female counterparts.

The separation of units by gender produces more inequalities, while also giving more power to one group. This is why the black female experience is crippled and looked at as absolute in the mainstream construct of how we look at movements and abuse that black people face. These intraracial issues need to demolished and elucidated without us as black men being cantankerous about these changes that need to be made. Men should never assume we are losing something by giving power to women. We can't only acknowledge blackness when a male face is at the forefront of the movement or when it's a male face being oppressed. By ignoring our sisters, institutions begin to make these practices natural, and they become enacted into the fabric of society in subtle ways that are easily hidden, but prominent.

We must quantify our appreciation for women in public like we do our men, and we must do it without expecting an award for doing what is morally expected. We can't look at it as criminal to ask black men to recognize black women in the midst of struggle because it may come off as divisive. By doing that, it is critical to note that we are deeming black women second-class citizens. Black men must not be looked at as being seated first class in the plane of struggle, because when the plane crashes, everyone dies. We must allow these fresh ideas of femininity to live inside their own dreams. We must birth possibilities and impregnate them with new ideas. When black men are fighting for the lead and control, we are doing a disservice to the movement by only caring about the image on the front page. Sometimes when we preach change with black men as the focal point, we allow black women to stay indebted, whether it's in the fight against police brutality, education, the prison industrial complex, or poverty.

Once you devalue her life, you devalue yourself, because she is responsible for your life. Society will not advance until we stop and realize that we need to praise and have a pragma type of love for the women who not only birthed us, but the women who birthed this world.

CHAPTER 21

Dear Young Brother

Dear Young Brother,

I'm writing you another letter, with the intent of apologizing and speaking to you more in-depth on the plight of black males. My previous letter sort of came off pretentious and out of touch with your current predicament. Even though I was someone who lived in the hood per se, I wasn't a person who was of the hood. Too often we get so caught up in our own narcissistic ignorance, we feel that once we obtain a miniscule amount of knowledge, we now hold the key to unlock the pathologies that are detrimental to people in the underserved communities.

I can read the works of Dubois, Malcolm, King, and many others, but having knowledge of those individuals doesn't give anyone the copyright to author the doctrine that will alleviate suffering and the de facto laws that will build community. However, before challenging others we first listen to them to garner the perspective. Then we must gain their respect before adding our opinions. I see nothing wrong with challenging you to be better, but the challenges must come from the source of love and not vitriol. I will always challenge you, but I will not put you down, unless I'm providing an outstretched hand to pull you back up.

While I challenge you, I never want to come across as one of those upwardly mobile blacks who has this ideology predicated on parochialism and positive-thought materialism. Too often blacks who have no connection with these urban communities come in with this myopic view of progress, and they attempt to sell a lifestyle that ignores systemic issues that are prevalent in these areas. I, like you, wish that people would understand that leaders are birthed out of the struggle. They can't be presented to those within these deprived communities to lead when they haven't emerged out of these communities. The dominant society can't be allowed to pick our leaders. The streets must do that. Just because someone has a black face, that doesn't mean that person has black interests in mind. I understand that you are frustrated with the countless mantras of respectability politics—the same politics that profess that prosperity will come once you pull your pants up, change your name to one that is acceptable to whiteness, and adjust your clothing attire to make you look less criminal. Since our last letter we have had countless victims who were targeted and shot down because they didn't fit the mold of upstanding young black men. I never want you to end up like Tray, Mike, Walter, Freddie, or the other infinite names of people who were killed with little to no recall. Even if you changed your image, that still doesn't erase the hatred people may have for you.

Too often those who ascribe to positive-thought materialism think that if we live right, pray right, and think right, we will be rewarded by a life filled with happiness. I want the best for you, but I never want you to ignore the social injustices and dilapidation that happen in your community while going unchecked.

Dear Young Real Nigga, I have a fecundity of hope that you will excel beyond measure and that you will surpass the places that people have destined you for without even knowing your name. I just ask that you never forget where you came from and still remain the same real nigga that you claim to be. Real is never going against your core beliefs, always maintaining a stature that is to be respected, and always maintaining a moral conscience.

As I close this letter to you, I must express (out of love) that too often the narrative is to get up out of the hood instead of trying to build it up. Simply moving out isn't enough. Living in middle-income communities is normal to most Americans. Strive for better. Praising normalcy is basically saying that we are content with mediocrity. Always remember that grass is normal. We must stop using green grass as a ceiling for achievement. We as black people are playing catch-up. We must muster the courage to do better and to provide opportunities for those who look up to us.

I never want to shun you, but I want to help build you up. No matter if you are reading this in a school library, detention center, prison, or simply off a blog site, just know that somebody loves you, and don't ever think that you are in this world alone.

Love,

Brandon C. Lovelace

CHAPTER 22

A Black Monster

O ctober 2, 1995, is a date that will forever be in the consciousness of many Americans who were old enough to remember: the trial of "People of the State of California v. Orenthal James Simpson." This was more than a murder trial that starred OJ Simpson in the arena of the court juxtaposed to the football stadium in which he was normally known to suit up for. That trial had all the elements for a championship event: race, stardom, glamour, big-name lawyers, and a relationship saga. Your favorite scriptwriters in Hollywood can only dream of a storyline like this one.

The murder of Nicole Simpson, a woman who happened to be white, amplified persistent racial tensions when OJ Simpson was accused. Even though OJ was later acquitted, people still have questions on whether or not he was factually innocent.

Even though many would consider OJ to be the quintessential definition of a man who attempted to walk a post-racial tightrope, not by denying his blackness, but by avoiding it at all costs, race was still an overbearing factor during this case. OJ would perspicuously express that he identified being a black man, but he was not restricted by it. Even though the hegemonic US society expresses this notion of being post-racial, this case let us know that it simply was a false utopia of race relations in this country, especially with the darkened image of OJ on *Times* magazine's cover that was published. Black men have historically been accused of harming white women, in regards to murder, rape, and other various forms of assault. Historically, stories such as Amanda Knox, Emmitt Till, Susan Smith, George Stinney, Charles Stuart, and many others come to mind. The belief that black men are boogeymen and white women are damsels in distress was on the conscience of many black Americans.

Even though a slew of mixed reactions over the incident were evident, many in the black community finally felt that the acquittal of OJ was a form of restorative justice for a people who not only were lynched on trees, but also lynched in courtrooms. The sense of "We finally won" was expressed from living rooms, pool halls, and barbershops across the United States. Even though one trial could not make up for countless times that the legal system has failed blacks, this one trial was amazing grace for many. Even though I was only six years of age, I still remember watching this trial in my grand-mother's living room and hearing commentary from family about how the legal system was against us. Even though I wasn't cognizant of the politics of race, this moment could be looked at as a starting point, when I recognized how different it was to be black and male in the United States.

Whether it's regarding incidents with high-profile black men such as Kobe Bryant or Jamal (from the block), once issues of interracial and gender violence intersect, an array of concerns and theories begin to suffice. Black men are stereotypically viewed as dangerous and hypersexual; when we live in a world with these myopic bigoted views, many in black communities automatically look at the instances within a parochial lens as a proverbial modern-day social lynching.

As a youth I frequently heard the saying, "If she can't use your comb, don't bring her home." As an adult I began to realize that it wasn't said as a proclivity to date black women, but it was used as a warning of the dangers that many blacks felt were imminent in regards to dating white women. I've encountered many white ladies whom I consider friends and all-around good people, but I still have this innate amicable fear of white women who are strangers to me. I refuse to get on elevators with them, and I avoid any type of interaction with them that can be perceived as sexual. Even though my avoidance of white women sexually is used as a defense mechanism, even that couldn't save me from being King Kong or the black boogeyman.

In the middle of one summer, I spent a cumulative amount of time totaling six weeks in a town outside of Omaha, Nebraska learning about social welfare. There I was surrounded by several people who lived in big cities and smaller towns. During my breaks in-between training material, I made a conscious effort to read a book. One of the persons in my class saw a book I was reading entitled *The Possessive Investment in Whiteness*. I was accused of being racist. Even though I was never addressed by these allegations directly from the individual, several people came up to trying to get an inside scoop regarding my views. The irony of it all was that the author, George Lipsitz, is a white man. I was not ashamed of the book I was reading, nor did I feel a sense of guilt for the reactions that others may have had, but I was glad it impregnated others in the training class with a sense of urgency to talk, listen, and be honest about white privilege and how whiteness is protected. I thought after the duration of this six weeks, I would have been rid of the individual involved, but our paths crossed again in an office in Omaha doing work for the community at large.

On one particular day I was having one of my usual conversations with a friend of mine during lunch. This conversation reared into the topic of sex work, primarily how blacks view sex work. Even though this topic contains a proliferation of nuances that usually go hidden, sex work is usually seen through a myopic prism of black and white, instead of the blurred gray areas that exist. Since I was talking to a friend in an informal setting, a slew of colloquialisms were used to advance our conversation on this topic. But when you mix the perception of black hypersexuality, prejudgments, and one who falls outside the linguistic capacity of black vernacular, one may feel that they are interpreting something lucidly, but they may be hearing it through their class, race, gender, tradition, or even their bigotry. One conversation I unconsciously disregarded moments after I hung up from a call with my friend resulted in one of the biggest fears for a black man.

On an afternoon weekday I returned to my home after attending a job fair at a local hotel, and I heard my apartment buzzer blare in succession. This was very peculiar because no one ever rings my buzzer. Whenever I have visitors, they always call to tell me they are outside or pulling up. I initially thought someone pressed the wrong apartment number, but I briskly walked down three flights of stairs. I could only imagine that my face resembled that of a deer caught in the space of a pair of headlights when I saw three police officers at my door as I'm dressed in a wife-beater and a pair of suit pants.

Even though police brutality has been a sustaining occurring issue, it has been sensationalized since the death of Mike Brown by the gun of Darren Wilson. One could imagine the fear I had seeing these officers on my front porch. They initially asked if I knew why they were there, but I let them know of my obliviousness to their visit. After a few minutes of us going back and forth, they ask whether I was an active participant in any sex trafficking. We have this racial incivility perception about black people, in which they are looked at as less than human and nonobsequious. With the lack of trust that exists among many blacks and law enforcement, I had to take a temporary moratorium on how felt law enforcement viewed me so I could plead my innocence. I feel that this occurred because of my consternation, which developed because of the accusations that was presented to me and the news that was broadcast on local news networks.

These accusations were particularly troubling because a few days prior, the federal government, in conjunction with local police departments, busted a large number of pimps, prostitutes, and customers in a large sting. This wasn't the first bust, but just another bust in a long line of arrests that had occurred over a number of years. Anger didn't initially encompass me. I was more in a state of fear. As I proceeded to clear my name from these accusations, I was very shaken in the same manner as if I were being pulled over by the police. Many feel that any encounter with the police can result in death for a black person. I'm always filled with ambiguous thoughts. Even though normal encounters may seem innocuous, as a black person the fear that you can be arrested or convicted for something you didn't do is always an axiomatic feeling.

From the time we are cognizant of what it means to be black, blacks have perspicacious ideals of how we tend to get the short end of the criminal justice stick. These statements may seem hyperbolic in reality, but this is a constant fear that many of us have in this day and age. This is not to perpetuate the notion that cops are actively searching for blacks to arrest and mendacious when it comes to encounters with blacks, but blacks akin to criminals within the unconscious belief of a world that sees blackness are less than the hegemonic standard. Even though we have activists, we are full-fledged in the work of fighting against oppression. The standard is still very apodictic in how blacks navigate through these systems.

We are taught that we shouldn't speak about certain accusations without a lawyer present, but my innate fear of being criminalized persuaded me to allow these officers to look at photos in my phone and to search my car. Luckily, the officers told me they didn't see anything that suggested that I was involved in any type of operation, so they told me I was good.

Even though I never doubted my innocence, just the mere thought of having everything that I worked for destroyed due to this belief of black men being the boogeyman and hypersexualized was very much disconcerting to my normal phlegmatic demeanor.

My incident didn't gain much attention outside my front porch. Even though I have strong opinions about how blacks are regarded within the legal system, this incident didn't promote any abhorrent feelings toward the individuals who questioned me. But it deepened my disgust and rancor for how easy it is to accuse people like me of heinous crimes. After the police left, I still felt an inhibition about being open about this incident because I felt that every move I was making was being watched.

Whether you're OJ Simpson, Emmitt Till, George Stinney, or even me, you can still be suspected of harming a white woman, even if your image is that of a stereotypical black man or someone who is perceived to be post racial. The sword that knights you will be the same one that is used to good-night you.

I still have this fear of getting on elevators with lone white women. This incident didn't put more aggressive invidious thoughts in my head about all white women, because I know several who have shown me that this notion of racial harmony isn't farfetched or impossible. But I know the road is still a long one to be traveled.

CHAPTER 23

THE RELATIVE DEPRIVATION IN FERGUSON

Let the ruling classes tremble at a Communist revolution. The proletarians have nothing to lose but their chains. They have a world to win.

—Karl Marx, 1848

Marx believed that the people at the bottom would rise because of absolute deprivation. Many would oppose that idea and would be more inclined to deal with relative deprivation, especially in social oppression that doesn't solely focus on economic oppression. Marx believed that once those at the bottom (proletariat) were at the point of receiving the maximum amount of oppression from the bourgeoisie, only then would they band together to rise up. We can't really blame Marx for not taking into account his thoughts on absolute deprivation when his Communist Manifesto dealt with mainly economics instead of social movements.

Many people around the world are watching what is unfolding and has unfolded in Ferguson, Missouri, after the death of a young man named Michael Brown. All life is precious, but he's just like Eric Garner, Ezell Ford, and countless others whose lives were ended by law enforcement. Even though these men were unarmed, they were killed—not because individually they may have posed a threat, but because black humanity is not valued in a country that initially brought them here as commodities.

People in Ferguson are not just protesting and rioting over the death of one child, but over decades of frustration with the local police department in St. Louis County, where you have a group that has been eviscerated from traditional American experience and made to look at themselves as subhuman not worthy of social equality.

Even though the city is comprised up of mainly African American residents (66 percent), the mayor and five-sixths of the city council members are white. Even though the population figures give off the notion of a strong black structure within the city, this is simply not true. The city still retains a white power structure even though it isn't reflected in the citizens that it governs. When incidents like this occur, elected officials are not in tune with the concerns of their citizens. The police force is also not reflective of the people. The force has fifty-three individuals on its roster, but only three are black.

People in black communities, males especially, already have a disdain for law enforcement, which can be attributed to their legacy of brutality and racial profiling among blacks. Even though we can pinpoint "good" officers, the institution of law enforcement is rooted in oppression of people of color.

The killing of Michael Brown is the straw that broke the camel's back, a sentiment that many black residents in the area might allude to. A community deprived of a dream they bought from the country they reside in finally became fed up and stood together in solidarity with more than hope. They rose up and demanded justice, not just for Mike Brown, but for the racial tension that the county has been plagued with over the years. These leading events brought on the protest and the revolution that we are witnessing now, which can be explained by the theory of relative deprivation.

James C. Davies thought of social movements when it came to revolutions. He created the J Curve, which deals with rising expectations that explain why Marx's theory didn't support the reasons for why the oppressed would get involved in social protest and movements, instead of positioning themselves in roles of social and political activists. Davies argues with his J Curve model that people will rise up to join social causes after periods of gradual improvement in the economy start to slow down. Even though economic prosperity is slowing down or decreasing the people's expectations for where they should be at in life, those hopes and aspirations continue to escalate (Davies 1962).

This curve shows how we get into the theory of relative deprivation.

Relative deprivation, in hindsight, is the understanding that you are being deprived of something that you believe wholeheartedly you should be entitled to. People will start to look at those around them who have considerably more than them and will soon become discontented with where their lives are (Walker & Smith 2001). Relative deprivation doesn't only deal with economics, but it also includes political and social deprivation. The perception of relative deprivation has dire consequences for behavior and attitudes, including feelings of stress, political attitudes, and participation in collective action. The theory was founded by Robert Merton, but one of the first formal and widely used definitions came from Walter Runciman, who used four points to argue his interruption of Merton's theory.

1. Person A does not have X.
2. Person A knows of other persons that have X.
3. Person A wants to have X.
4. Person A believes obtaining X is realistic (Runciman 1966).

Those citizens of Ferguson don't have the law on their side like other residents, so they understand the feeling of disenfranchisement in regards to what they believe they deserve. People will feel outraged and will have the sense of urgency to come together as a collective once they feel they are being denied justice, upward mobility to a higher status, or even privilege. That is what happened to those residing in Ferguson and others who can understand the rage of the overpolicing of a community who feel racially harassed by the police. These people live in a nation where every twenty-eight hours a black is killed by the police or a vigilante. Marx argued about absolute deprivation, which states that people react merely off of just negative conditions. The Relative Deprivation Theory argues that people react over what they feel they should have.

Political scientist Ted Robert Gurr gave three values in his book *Why Men Rebel*, arguing his point on different values that a man needs to be content and what happens when he is placed at a disadvantage in obtaining or maintaining those values. They included welfare values, interpersonal values, and power values. Welfare values included those that make physical contributions to life; interpersonal included those that directly correlated with satisfaction received from nonauthoritative interactions; and power values spoke of our environment influencing our behavior (Gurr 1970). Gurr wrote on page 58, "Men are quick to aspire beyond their social means and quick to anger when those means prove inadequate, but slow to accept their limitations." When a man sees that he isn't achieving the same level of affluence in society, Gurr argues that biologically he gets to where he needs justification for this. This justification usually leads to blaming different organizations, whether it's a school system, government institution, or business. Sometimes those who are placing blame will place it on prominent individuals within those organizations. Once you place this blame on others, you are essentially becoming a victim of decremental deprivation, which basically means you are placing the fault on other things that are taking away from your own opportunity of equality.

Gurr's last value, which was interpersonal, called for status, communality, and ideational coherence—which is important so that people can have a sense of identity. Those in Ferguson and across the United States are denied that opportunity because black has become synonymous with bad. Gurr also writes in *Why Men Rebel* about the notions of aspiration, progressive, and detrimental deprivation and how each can result in the gathering of frustrated people to help form a social movement.

CHAPTER 24

The Mark of Cain

In the book of Genesis, more specifically in the fourth chapter, the story of Cain and Abel can be found. This pericope offers a historical Christian perspective of the first murder. Whether you are a follower or not, this poignant story offers a type of signification that can loosely be found in modern-day social contexts.

Within this story we can see the relationship between Cain and how we view felons and those who have been tainted with a prison record, and more importantly how the word *criminal* has now become synonymous with *black*. Being a black man in what many consider the free world feels at times as though my existential being is encamped inside a panopticon.

Cain was the jealous brother, according to Christian and even Islamic scripture, who ended up killing his brother Abel because he was dissatisfied that his offering was rejected, while his brother's was accepted. The moral of the story is about jealousy, and an underlying hermeneutical message is the mark of Cain that was initiated by GOD. I feel that this signification is important within a global context because now we live amid the modulation of white supremacy and punishment.

Many prominent activists and scholars such as Angela Davis, Marc Lamont Hill, Nils Christie, Michelle Alexander, Cornel West, and Thomas Mathiesen have committed great portions of their lives and work to teaching and to eradicating the views of how we not only view crime, but also how we treat those who are trapped inside the system.

One Thursday night during a lecture from Angela Davis at the local Holland Center in Nebraska, she spoke on the work many activists are doing to "remove the box" from job applications. This is very important because in many states, that box asks potential employees if they have ever been convicted of a felony, or in some instances a crime. We look at the mark of Cain; it was given for two reasons. The first was because he committed a murder against his brother, and the second was because he lied to GOD about the killing. The mark on Cain was a sign for others not to cause him harm because they too would feel the wrath of GOD, but it is also believed that this curse prevented Cain from yielding farmland from crops, which forced him into living a nomadic lifestyle.

When we look at the dichotomy of persons with criminal records and the story of Cain, a correlation exists between Cain's inability to yield crops and the inability of those with records to find sustaining employment. Of course there are always expectations. For instance, you wouldn't want someone convicted of child molestation to work in a child-care center because of the danger and consequences of what recidivism could mean. However, when you put the box on job applications, an employer might say it's a mechanism to weed out bad employees, but in reality it works as a machination to prevent rehabilitation of those who have paid their debts to society with a check that has been cleared. Once you emasculate a person from obtaining an adequate wage, you are in a sense forcing that person into living a nomadic life like that of Cain, where that person will be placed amid temptations that increases the chance of recidivism.

In most instances, having the mark as a criminal taints many from being able to improve their situation so they can function freely in society. Instead, it places them in a caste system where they are looked at as alien citizens. Many of the rights that were promised to them in the US Constitution are taken away, and they become a visitor in a country that they've inherited from birth. They now are actors in a play of life that they have not written, directed by a system of individuals they don't know. In many instances it blocks their ability to vote, to sit as jurors, and to possess firearms. And like I've stated earlier, it initiates a de facto form of segregation in the form of employment. Some may even consider this the new Jim Crow, which is also the title of the groundbreaking book by Michelle Alexander.

In her book Michelle Alexander discusses how the prison industrial complex compromises the rights of people, mainly those from poor communities who happen to be black and brown men. Now we also see a rise of women who are falling into these same vicious traps as well. With black and brown disproportionality populating the cells, we begin to apply shade to what we envision criminals to resemble.

Earlier I claimed that as a black man, I felt like I was trapped in a panopticon. A panopticon was created by an English philosopher and social theorist named Jeremy Bentham. It was originally an institutional structure that allowed watchmen to observe prisoners. The thing about this invention is that while the watchman is afforded the ability to watch prisoners, the prisoners can't see him. On any given day, they don't know whether he's watching or not, but the idea of someone watching them is effective because the perceived threat is always persistent. Even though his design was never completed, several structures that were built off his idea were put in place in a few places around the world. This idea has received criticism mainly due to how inhumane it comes across in the way we think of inmates. However, we can see the idea of panopticons in stores, institutions, and other places with security cameras. Even though we are unaware if we are being watched, the possibility is enough in most cases. I argue that I feel like I'm in one because just like the mark of Cain and the coloring of criminals, I feel as though I am always initially perceived to be a problem, or troublesome.

As a black man in the United States, I feel as if my every move is being watched meticulously, because at times it seems like my room for error is that of an inch. All I ever wanted to be in life was an American, but an honest one.

However, the core values of what it means to be an American have been diluted. One earned his slice of pie, but he shared it with those who may have miscalculated or inadvertently messed up the recipe.

However, to be an honest American, it seems that if you don't fit the cookie-cutter reflection of the American man, you somehow are given one strike. Even though my criminal history is marginal; the only things on my record are minor traffic tickets. Even though I have friends who have navigated through the criminal justice system, I can see the pain, strife, and degradation they experience as they try to capture an American dream that is seemingly out of the grasp of their fingertips. I'm optimistic in a sense because I truly believe that everyone has a shot, but some have lay-ups, others get an elbow shot, many are afforded a three-point shot, and too many seem to get a half-court shot.

However, once we look at the intersectionality of being black and with a criminal record, that shot now becomes one from full court. I don't say this to come off as though I shouldn't be judged because of the mistakes other black have made, even though I do find it problematic that we are viewed within a myopic monolithic lens. I believe no one's livelihood should be revoked because of actions made in the past. Every time I see someone struggling with this mark of Cain, I picture myself being in that person's position. Like all people, I've made mistakes that could have put me in that position, but I was lucky. Too often we feel as though we can't be empathic to situations that we have don't have a direct context with.

The issue with these preconceived notions is that not only do they discriminate on the basis of race and class, but these discriminations and prejudices emasculate segments of the population, reproducing inequalities in communities of collapse and dilapidation. Being black seems as though it's part of an unwritten white supremacist interpolation that says blacks go to the proverbial back of the line. This mark of Cain has decimated generations of communities, based on a predisposition of what a criminal looks like. This way of thinking or treatment makes many black people look suspect when that person doesn't appeal to the unequal standards placed on them by the hegemonic power structure.

This way of visually perceiving criminality begins to create a construct of respectability politics within the constraints of black people—not just in the sense of dress and verbiage, but also in a sense of class. It seems as the younger black, educated millennial class is now at odds with the older black educated class who witnessed the civil rights struggle. Whenever we speak of respectable politics, these two groups are usually at the forefront of the battlefield. However, it seems as though the poor people get left out of these conversations. Even they are used by people working on analytical studies, or they get beat up on by the basis of black meritocracy. Instead of confronting the most powerful, we begin to scapegoat the most vulnerable. People in general and especially black people are not monotonous inside the basis of race. They should not only be valued equally, but it also should be known that all of us are looked at as the same outside these communities.

A continuous understanding needs to be adjudicated among us to garner a puritanical concept of inclusiveness about our plight to cleanse ourselves of the mark of Cain. Kendrick Lamar was bombarded with backlash when he questioned the lack of outrage regarding black-on-black killings in comparisons to the killing of Trayvon Martin. Even though on the surface it may seem problematic and dismissive of racial motivations, it does allow us to examine things below the surface level. He comes from a community like many of ours that have been plagued with gentrification, police killings, underfunding of education, and a plethora of other things, but when we begin the process of accretion, we become stronger in our fight. We haven't seen groups of gangs coming together for one cause since the beating of Rodney King. Once we realize that the common enemy isn't a street corner or an alternative color, we can begin a greater fight against the system.

Even though destroying property within a community can be problematic, especially if those businesses hire an abundance of people from the communities in which they are located. However, those gangs and members became one. When you operate in a form of separatism among a local community, you begin to reproduce more inequalities, which in turn gives greater power to the dominant hegemonic power structure. Although the riot that followed the acquittal of the officers who beat Rodney King supported the faulty narrative of blacks being vile and violent, it also was a direct example of relative deprivation theory that was theorized by Robert K. Merton. This was a direct response to sociological implications of urban dislocations and poverty-bred crime. We have several leaders with a community who argue that we must be peaceful in response to injustice, but I would argue that exhibiting the threat of not backing down to an oppressor is a better call for action to bring about peace to a historically unwilling compromiser.

In regards to washing away this mark of Cain, we must decide what's more obscene: the actions or words we use, or the situations we confront head on.

CHAPTER 25

Darkness on Omaha's North Side

I see more needles with dried, dark-red blood in the street than kids happily playing in them.

Babies crying for food and mothers crying oceans because they don't have the means to feed them.

Schools are closing yearly, but prisons seem like they are opening daily.

Cost of living is skyrocketing, but social funds are plummeting.

I just want to be a lawyer, a scientist, or somebody with a PhD, but I'm six foot three, and my community says I should try to live out hoop dreams.

I have more access to a ball court than a library.

I see more despair than hope, more junkies and crack fiends than people who look like me living out million-dollar dreams, swiping black cards for expensive things.

Gentrification, felonies, kids misdiagnosed with mental retardation, but a lack of youth leading my country to become a better nation.

Will I overcome or just become another statistic stuck at the bottom?

Either my people are dying, or they are clocking in nine to fives and ten to sixes, minimum wage living at sixty-three because seventy for us is when we are retiring.

Not because they want to, but to keep the heat on and to give Junior a couple presents for Christmas.

Streetlights are shining like thousand-watt light bulbs, but those are the only things bright on Omaha's north side.

Mothers cry, their babies die, and children wonder why.

They wonder why it has to be like this.

Sometimes we just want to see our side shine, brighten up our day like the Woodmen Tower's bright lights.

But no, we walk in darkness on Omaha's North Side, looking for hope that the former senator and our current president promised us, but no one can see the pain, because the sun doesn't shine on the north side.

Made in the USA
Columbia, SC
30 March 2018